Refined Suga

Memoir of a Storyteller

by Lynne M. Moore

Author's Note: This book was written from memory and from what records I had available to me. The conversations all come from my recollections; and not written to represent word-for-word transcripts. Rather, I have retold them in a way that evokes the feeling and meaning of what was said and, in all instances, the essence of the dialogue is accurate.

Book Layout by Linda Hurley
Cover Design by Bob Hurley

This book is dedicated to
Pauline Nunez Moore for asking me to write this story but
to wait until AFTER she had passed on,
and to
Mignon "Missy" Mouton who will NEVER be gone from our hearts.

Prologue

New Orleans in the thirties, I'm told, was a haven for the well-heeled and titled; a class system engraved in every consciousness. An abundance of flowering vines climbed to third-story lace balconies along St. Charles Avenue. Streetcars ran on the grassy median where miles of tracks passed a hundred mansions reminiscent of European royalty. This enchanted area is still known as 'The Garden District', famous for its ambiance and hauntings, occupied now by generations of patrician families. The fragrances of lush gardenias, roses and bougainvillea reach the senses like the bouquet of fine wine. Some say you could smell money there!

Those uptown were wealthy and privileged, while downtown, below Canal Street, was an ethnic melting pot, inhabited by blue-collar immigrants working at menial jobs. On the riverfront Negro spirituals and foghorns competed with the bona fide musicians, in the Vieux Carrè, the French Quarter, who played all night, slept all day, and lived on drugs, chicory coffee and hand-rolled smokes. Long sleeves covered evidence of illegal drugs, as weary bodies shuffled in the wee hours through dark alleyways where they flopped on stained mattresses in dismal garrets. Nightly a paddy wagon picked up derelicts and drunks sleeping in doorways and deposited them at the jail. Gutters flowed with refuse, urine and at times, blood and vomit; a stench that has been part of the Vieux Carrè, for three hundred years. Water wagons sprayed streets daily, the effluent carried to the river via a brick ditch in Pirates' Alley between the Cathedral and the Cabildo.

Although I was fortunate enough to be reared by refined and well-to-do grandparents, I have always questioned my parentage because of what I've been told or overheard. My childhood was fraught with innuendo, accusation, and hints of my mother's shame. I wonder now why I was afraid to ask more questions.

Acknowledgments

My sincere thanks to the following individuals who have been so instrumental in the completion of my 30-year struggle to commit my story to paper.

To Linda Hurley, the ultimate editor, who knows what I mean even when I don't say it properly and who makes sure that my 'facts' are really "facts".

To Bob Hurley for his cover design and superior skill in restoring my old photographs.

My late uncle, Leroy Mayeux, Sr., who provided the photograph for the cover which I had never seen before. He kept it safe for 75 years.

Sammie Mouton and Dr. Peter Mouton; and Suzanne Lindley and Dr. Keith Lindley who provided encouragement and invaluable input.

Thank you to readers Grace Young, Sue Maley, Leslie Mouton, Alex Lindley, Jane Clites, Sylvia Davis, Phyllis Story and Vera Reif who gave me their insight.

Thank you to Mary Ann Revel of Lake Sumter State College who believed in me.

Finally, Frank Mouton is to be congratulated for his detailed memory of places, names, and dates; and his fortitude in letting me reveal the details of our journey.

Peace be with you all.

Chapter 1

The Sarrats, my grandparents, were direct descendants of Andrès Almonaster y Rojas, who was born of a noble Andalusian family in 1724 in Mairena del Alcor, Spain. In 1769 he arrived in Louisiana, called "the Indies" by Europeans; his position was that of alcade (mayor or chief magistrate). He was ultimately made Knight of the Royal and Distinguished Spanish Order of Carlos III in 1796; an honor, which among other privileges, called for him to be referred to as "his excellence".

Pierre, Henriette Marie, George ~ Circa 1893

Moving forward three generations to April 1891, Pierre Louis Sarrat was born into high society, second son of Henriette Marie Andrès and George Antoine Sarrat, Sr., a wealthy cotton broker. Pierre's brother, George, then two years old, began to speak with a slight stutter which he never overcame. These handsome boys were privately educated by French tutors through sixth grade, where they read the classics, learned English, German, mathematics, a wealth of geography and history, and were also thoroughly versed in manners and protocol by Henriette. As they grew older, afternoons were spent riding their own horses or at the race track. George liked to gamble most evenings, while Pierre preferred the opera house or dancing at the homes of friends.

In 1911, when George announced his intention to court Marie Haydee Michel, his father suggested he complete his studies while engaging the young lady for the required two-year courtship. Marie Haydee's youngest sister, Marie Josephine, at the age of fourteen, was to chaperone the couple on their rounds of parties, picnics and the theater.

Henriette volunteered George's brother, Pierre to escort the younger, comely Michel girl. He cooperated, reluctantly. "Mignon" was her nickname, meaning 'cute and little' she was easily the most beautiful of the four Michel girls. Her black curls and pleasant smile, not to mention a mischievous twinkle in her dark eyes, soon won Pierre's heart.

Shortly after George and Marie Haydee's marriage in 1913, Pierre proposed to Mignon when she was just sixteen and preparing to make her debut. Her coming-out was abruptly cancelled when she accepted his ring. The couple married on 12 November 1914 at Holy Name of Jesus Church on St. Charles Avenue, with the crème de la crème of New Orleans society in attendance.

Marie Josephine Alpuente and Victor Edouard Michel, Mignon's parents, insisted the newlyweds move into their spacious home on what is now Governor Nicholls Street. Victor was sales manager of Henderson Sugar Refinery, well known and respected in sugar circles throughout the South. Mignon's eldest sister, Louise Clemonce de Leaumont, husband Walter and their six children and personal servants were already in residence there.

Marie Josephine (Mignon) Michel
Age 16

Dapper, charming Pierre was already a prominent figure in the New Orleans Cotton Exchange when, in September 1915, Mignon gave birth to their first son, Donald Michel, and the following October, a daughter, Germaine Marie. Within two years, Marie Josephine, died peacefully in her sleep leaving her two daughters to manage the house for their father.

Tragically, in 1919, Louise died in childbirth while her eighth baby, Michel, survived. Unable to face the future without her, Walter came to a violent end, when in despair, he took a gun to his head on the second anniversary of his wife's death. The *New Orleans Times-Picayune* article on 21 November 1921 reported, "Father Shoots Self After Morning Kiss of His Eight Tots When the last of his eight small children had romped out of his room after kissing him "good morning", Walter Leaumont, 39, well known cotton man, shot himself through the right temple at 7:45 o'clock Monday morning".

Suddenly, Pierre found himself in need of a large home to accommodate their four children, the eight Leaumont orphans (ranging in age from 2 to 9), Mignon's aging father, Pierre's parents, and a cadre of servants.

All were assembled, within a few months, for a Sunday afternoon ride to see where they would live. Mignon remained confined at home with her fifth pregnancy. The children tumbled out of five carriages faster than the attending help could control them. They stood transfixed, in awe of the new home Pierre had chosen.

Massive white columns graced the façade of the double plantation house, a mere thirty paces from the banks of Bayou Saint John. The right half of the home would house the Leaumonts and their servants, and with passages cut through on each level, the Sarrats and their attendants would occupy the left side.

Mignon delivered Lucille, Norman and Elise during her first three years in the new home. She soon grew disgruntled and maudlin, distanced from her stylish friends uptown in the Garden District. She envisioned her position in society threatened and her life finished at age twenty-four. Never giving Pierre a moment's peace, Mignon used every weapon, from silence, to pleading, to tears, reminding him constantly of her position in society, her birthright, and her sacrifices for him.

She related on many occasions, Pierre's attempt to impress her with the favorable features of their new locations. "Near here, ma coeur" he began, "are well-endowed estates and one of the most historic spots in City Park, the world famous "Dueling Oaks". This is the site of heroics of the most fascinating and courageous gentlemen of a bygone era. In early Creole days, more duels were fought here, in New Orleans, than any other place in America."

"Promise me," she responded, "you will not take part in any duels just because we are living near immortal oak trees!" Pierre smiled at her joke and kissed her hand. He settled the issue by concluding, "Men don't duel anymore, dearest, today men sue each other."

Meanwhile, in Chalmette, an intimate distance from the site of the Battle of New Orleans, in a somewhat less affluent neighborhood, lived the pure Creole Nunez family. The following accounts are recorded as they were told to me, in minute detail, by Pauline Angelle Nunez Moore, when she asked me to write this story. She was only sixteen when she was summoned to her parents' sitting room by her father, Adrion.

In a hushed voice, her father said, "Pauline, I have just admitted our cousin, William Moore, to the front parlor. He brings some startling news."

"News, Papa?" she drew her brows together in a frown.

"It seems his son, Andrew, confessed that he has experienced carnal knowledge of you, dear girl." Pauline then lowered her eyes; fighting back tears of anguish and guilt but said nothing.

"Well, I see," her father said, "then, this is true?" Adrion's expressive eyes displayed his displeasure.

"Yes, Papa," she whispered. "I am so sorry I didn't tell you myself. But why has he come here?"

Raising his voice, Nunez said, "Child, he has come to get you! He insists that you and Andrew marry immediately. Your mother and I agree, although it is not what we intended for you. We expected you to advance your education."

"Papa," she said eagerly, "Toby, is a fine man with a great future."

"You call him Toby?" he asked.

"Yes, Papa, his name is Andrew Given Tobias Moore. In business, he goes by his initials, 'AGT', but his friends just call him Toby."

"And is this what you want?" he asked.

At this point she felt she had no choice. "I'm sure it's best, if you and Mother agree." she said, "I suspect I am possibly with chil..."

At this point her father covered his eyes with one hand and said firmly, "Say no more, Pauline! Gather up your things. We shall not inconvenience Cousin William by making him wait any longer. His carriage is outside." She did as she was told.

Andrew was active in the forestry and lumber industries and an expert in railroads, giving speeches throughout the United States about transportation, as he carved a name for himself. He was also well respected for introducing southern pine to northern furniture factories. He was traffic manager of the Southern Pine Association and held a seat on the Board of Trade in both New Orleans and Gainesville,

Florida. He published two books, Forestry in the Lumber Industry and Opportunities for Foresters in the Southern Lumber Industry, both in 1941. He was also awarded an Honorary Degree by Tulane University.

In the aftermath of their impromptu Presbyterian wedding, Andrew made Pauline vow never to dance with another man as long as she lived, and to forego Catholicism.

His sisters' high esteem for Andrew resulted in their acceptance of her into their home. Eight months after the wedding, their baby son died in infancy. He was christened "Chalen" secretly by their Catholic Negro cook, Eva. She would again be prominent in Bruce and Germaine's story in 1916.

Pauline and Andrew were blessed with six more children and they developed an extensive estate in Jefferson Parish, a day-long carriage ride from New Orleans. Andrew stocked his stables with gentle mares for Pauline and the children, a massive Percheron to handle his 400 pounds, and together, on fine evenings, they rode along the levee of the Mississippi. He later installed a tennis court and the first privately-owned swimming pool in Jefferson Parish. He also commissioned a fifty-foot, double-ended yacht, which was christened "Wendy". It was berthed at West End, with access to the Gulf of Mexico through Lake Pontchartrain.

Andrew Tobias and Pauline Nunez Moore

But all the money in the world couldn't open society's doors for the nouveau riche Moores; doors available to the aristocratic Sarrats from birth. While their paths crossed occasionally at the Cabildo, along with other prominent men of their day, they moved in significantly different social circles.

Chapter 2

Franklin Delano Roosevelt was president, Ernest Hemmingway covered the Spanish Civil war from Madrid, and Seabiscuit amazed racing fans, during his five-year run. A loaf of bread cost $.08 and the average income was $1,713.00. Germaine Sarrat, 17, and Rosemonde Moore, 21, met while attending business school where Rose's brother, Bruce,17, was also studying bookkeeping and typing. The girls became fast friends despite their incongruent backgrounds.

Before long, Germaine set her cap for Bruce. He was tall, blonde, blue eyed and considered a dandy. Denied his company outside of school, she implored her parents to allow her to see Bruce socially, but her mother refused; insisting she concentrate on marrying 'high'.

Germaine constantly challenged both her parents and society's tenets. The Sarrats had been humiliated when she was expelled from St. Joseph Academy for hemming her uniform skirt above her knees and refusing to wear stockings or underwear. Her sisters and female cousins were subsequently withdrawn from the prestigious private school and transferred to public schools. Those cousins and sisters secretly admired her panache and affectionately nicknamed her "Germ".

As President of her Sorority, Omega Sigma, Germ received numerous social invitations. Bruce, a well-known playboy, wouldn't have given her a second glance, as she was stout and not particularly attractive, except for her gaining him admittance to dances and other functions.

Rose and Germ spent much of their free time at Dew Drop Inn, a honky-tonk in Jefferson Parish. Here, cheap contraband liquor, and dark trysts were the norm. According to her sisters, who loved to share stories of those days with me, even when I was very young, Germ encouraged Bruce's advances. She envisioned him as the means to escape her controlling mother and plotted to get him to marry her.

By his own admission, at 19, Bruce became bored with drinking and dancing and began looking for a career. Since he had regularly captained the 'Wendy', when Andrew entertained visiting dignitaries; his father encouraged him to join the Merchant Marine to further his maritime experience.

The Merchant ship's first anchorage was in Hawaii, where Bruce received a telegram from Germ saying he must come home, as she was 'in a family way'. He bitterly returned to New Orleans rather than disgrace his mother. Born on her twenty-fifth birthday, he was Pauline's favorite.

It was my grandparents' practice to take a walk after their dinner, for as long as I've known them. They strolled, admiring progress on roads, construction, and the new tall streetlamps adjacent to their estate. According to Germ and Bruce, they confronted them during one of their walks for the purpose of announcing their intention to marry.

"Mère and Papa," Germaine said nervously, "may I introduce Julius Bruce Moore?" The encounter ended badly when the Sarrats reiterated their dictum that Germaine was not to pursue any sort of relationship with Bruce, much less marriage. Germaine's response was to threaten the Sarrats with never seeing their first grandchild, not so subtly informing them of how far the relationship had already gone.

Rebuffed, Germ and Bruce returned to the Moore's home, while Andrew was away on business, asking Pauline for assistance. The patient and generous Pauline allowed Germ to share a room with Rose, who had confided in her mother that she was pregnant by her then current boyfriend, Charles Merriea. On the advice of her cook, Eva, Pauline's chauffer, Ed Ranegh, drove both girls to stay with a mid-wife in Mississippi until after the births.

Germaine Sarrat and Bruce Moore

Germ and Rose wrote to Bruce and Charles, respectively, in February, telling them that when they called to announce the births of their babies, the young men were to meet the L&N train at Carrollton, the last stop before New Orleans. From there the two couples would leave for Florida, never to face their parents again. The best laid plans...

They did get off the train in Carrollton, but there was only one baby and they never did escape to Florida. I was not to learn the truth behind that fiasco until I was eighteen years old.

The Sarrat's cook, Mary, and the baby nurse, Amélia Mollier, together with Effie Pilon, Mignon's personal maid, and Tomas, the butler/driver, related the events they witnessed concerning my unexpected arrival in the Sarrat household.

Pierre received a phone call, interrupting a dinner party in his home at 10 p.m. on the first of March 1936. "Who was that, dear?" Mignon demanded, her bejeweled right hand delicately raised to her diamond necklace, as was her habit.

"Never you mind, my dear, attend to our guests." Pierre said, as he excused himself. He then addressed the butler quietly, "Tomas, get the motorcar out and summon Amélia. Tell her to come along and to bring a small blanket."

Tomas brought the Packard to the rear entrance and instructed the nursemaid to sit in the back, while Père rode up front and directed him to drive to Baptist Hospital.

When they arrived, Tomas was told to wait, while Pierre hurried Amélia into the brightly lit, disinfectant-scented building. "I am Pierre Sarrat," he told the receptionist, "I received a call about an abandoned baby and was told my phone number was pinned to the baby's blanket. Whose baby is this?"

"I'm sorry, sir," the nurse replied, "we have no information except that the infant was left behind. She was not born here, she was just examined to make sure she was well, and the bill was not paid."

Pierre glimpsed at what appeared to be Germaine's handwriting on the note and, without a word, reached for his money clip. The nurse handed the baby over to Amélia, who wrapped her snugly and hurried out into the freezing night to the waiting car. Amélia and Tomas looked curiously at the newborn with pale eyelashes, sucking on nothing, sleeping peacefully. They said not a word when Père returned and ordered Tomas to drive home.

The guests had all departed by the time they returned. To prepare her mistress, Effie had told her of the trip to the hospital and the new arrival. Mignon, weeping, waited impatiently in her sitting room as Effie massaged her feet. Effie then busied herself in the background, eavesdropping, as Pierre settled himself in his armchair with a deep sigh.

"What were you thinking, Pierre?" Mignon cried.

"Beloved, understand, this could be our first grandchild. I could not allow the child to be turned over to an orphanage just because Germaine has acted foolishly. We can provide a home for the infant until she comes to her senses."

Mignon ranted, "What proof do you have that this child is Germaine's? Impulsive, selfish Germaine, who allowed that low class person to impregnate her just to embarrass me! What do you think of your daughter now?"

"When the time comes, I will see to it that Germaine's sin is annulled and welcome her home to care for her baby. Now relax, my dear, please don't let this upset you." Effie eased herself out through Mignon's dressing room and escaped into the shadows of the corridor.

The following day, Pierre ordered the help to retrieve a bassinet, high chair, and a child's chest of drawers from the attic, all of which required refinishing. They set to work with emery paper and white paint; with Tomas overseeing the project.

The three teenage girls, Hilda, Cyril, Lucille, plus twelve-year old Elise were joyful over the prospect of the new baby and argued about where she would sleep. Mignon settled the issue. "Girls, girls! Compose yourselves. Amélia will care for the baby as she did all of you. Not a word will be said outside the family, do you understand? When we reach Germaine, perhaps we can solve this mystery."

"Your Papa insists the baby will be christened on Sunday. Hilda, you will be the nannan, your brother, Donald, will be parrain. The laundress is freshening up the christening gown you've all worn. You will resume your studies now. Remember who you are and what we expect of you."

On Sunday, after mass, Pierre assembled the entire Leaumont clan along with his own children (with the exception of Germaine) at the baptismal font in the rear of Holy Rosary Church, Father Arginela officiating. Hilda, eighteen, held the baby who was wearing a bonnet larger than a dinner plate, swathed in a batiste and lace baptismal gown, so long it hung below Hilda's knees. I was christened 'Lynne Marie.'

Pierre's benevolence knew no bounds. Sixteen children from age twenty to zero were now in his care. His cheeks were surely aglow with pride as he tipped his hat to the ladies outside the church, as they headed home. At high noon, as the church bells pealed the Angelus, the help stood shoulder to shoulder, from the curb to the front door of the Sarrat residence; two columns of starched white shirts and aprons, a proud reception committee. The entire walkway was bordered with blossoming pink and white azaleas as the family ambled to the front door. Amélia, holding the door open received the baby from Hilda. There had not been an infant in the house in over a decade.

Chapter 3

In the service alley, the boisterous song of a street vendor distracted a chauffeur who was polishing a lustrous, new black 1939 Packard. “I got b’nanna, apple n’ peach, fine ripe t’mato n’ greens! I got de mangoes n’ cel’ry! I’m Rufus, here, I brings you da freshest!” A mule-drawn produce wagon laden with colorful vegetables and fruit came to a halt a few feet from Tomas, the chauffer, who wiped his right hand on his apron, extending it to the old man holding the mule’s reins.

“Eh, Rufus, ma ole’ friend, how you been?”

“Tomas! Comment ça va?”

“Très bien, et toi?”

“You still workin’ fo’ da Sarrat fam’ly?” Rufus inquired.

“Absolument! M. Sarrat, he reward me good!”

Our cook slipped out of the kitchen door to pick through the produce on the old man’s wagon. The sun cast a brilliant glow on her sparkling white uniform in high contrast to her gleeful black face. Using coins retrieved from an apron pocket, she paid for her selections. Satisfied with her string bag filled with cabbages and carrots, the plump black cook took notice of me perched on a low, whitewashed stone wall, my feet crossed nicely, as I had been taught. I was watching Tomas.

She snatched up my hand. “C’mon, child,” the woman scolded, “you s’posed to stay in da house. Come wit Mary.”

“She ain’t doin’ nuthin’ wrong, Mary. I keeps a’ eye on her.” Tomas defended me.

“Yeah, Tomas, but if Madame see her doin’ anythin’ she don’ like, that chile be out on da street. She din’t want her no how, so we bees extra careful wit her.”

“Au revoir, Tomas,” I called back to him as Mary led me up the steps and through the kitchen door. Tomas waved, and I gave a little wave back, then turned my full attention to the cook.

“Why can’t I stay outside, Mary?” I asked.

“If y’know whass good f’you, you be in da house wit me or Amélia. Go climb up in yo’ tall chair and Mary give you a cracker.” She replied.

I climbed easily into the wicker high chair with the tray removed and Mary pushed it close to the table. The strong violet fragrance of Vetiver perfume announced the appearance of Mère as she came into the breakfast room, and in a harsh voice, confronted the cook. “Mary where has the child been? I looked in a moment ago and she was nowhere to be seen.”

“She bin wit me and Tomas, Madame,” answered Mary

“Now, Mary, I depend on you to keep her inside when she’s downstairs,” and then turning to me, “Do as I say, Lynne, there will be no crumbs left on the linen! You make too much work for the laundress. Remember, you must always be grateful to me for taking you in, because, you know, dear, nobody wanted you.”

I had not yet learned to harbor resentment, only filial piety.

Mary poured milk into my cup, but I didn’t drink until Mère left the room. Nibbling on my cracker, I stared at Shirley Temple’s image on the blue cup and whispered, “If you were a real girl I would play with you.” Wetting my finger with spit from my mouth, I picked up every cracker crumb on the linen cloth.

Tomas came in through the kitchen door, washed his hands and shrugged into his jacket. "Nearly sundown, going now to fetch M'sieur from the Cotton Exchange, need anything from the French Market, Mary? Would the little one like to ride along?"

"Oh, yes, Tomas, may I come?" I cried.

"Hush, chile, you don't go nowhere, you stays righ' here wit Mary. If dat cracker dint ruin yo dinner, I'll fix yo plate soon as ahm done whippin' de mèrengue for the dessert" she muttered. "Belle, she dint help me a lick t'day, she been too busy gettin' dem lace curtains wash'd 'n on the stretchers, cause yo Gran'Mère don't like fo doze parlor windas ta be undressed."

"Mary, why do you always stay in the kitchen?" I asked.

"Lord, chile, Mary bin in de kitchen, sence ah was a girl, sence yo Gran'folks got married! Yo Gran'folks weren't no mo' den kids theyselfs back in 1914, so dey mama hired all da help, includin' me!"

"Why are there no other children here, Mary?" I asked.

The black woman laughed. "Who you tink all yo aunties an' uncles an' couzains is? Dem's growed up chirren! Yo Aunt Elise ain't but twelve years ol'ler than you, Suga! I seen dem all birthed, one at a time, rhiat here in da house. Amélia an' all da up-stair-help done raise all dem chirren. Belle and me, we's jest kitchen wimmen."

"But Mary, where is my mother? Gran'mère says she was a bad girl and ran off with a bad man. Where is she, Mary? In my story books there is always a mother." I asked curiously.

"I jus' cain't say, baby girl. Mary jus' don' know. Look here, Suga, you want a taste of dis mèrengue?" asked Mary.

"No, thank you, but I'd like another cracker, please."

After the white topping was placed on four fat lemon pies, Mary called my attention to the sound of tires on gravel in the drive.

"Who dat comin' home, baby girl? Who you tink gonna come thru da door wit Tomas?" said Mary.

"It's Père!" I cried jubilantly, "my Papa is home!" Turning around, I quickly climbed down backwards from my tall chair and headed for his dark striped trousers in the doorway. Père saw me running and used his outstretched hands, patting air, urging me to slow down. Suddenly, I felt cold inside, hearing noise thumping in my head where the big pain was starting. Just as I got to him a layer of gravity dropped me to the floor, unconscious. I woke up in my bed with Amélia sitting beside me, as usual. Amélia had thin gray braids crossed on top of her head and pieces of broom straw in her earlobes to keep the holes from closing up when she wasn't wearing her church earrings. I never noticed that her skin was the color of chocolate milk. Her skirts swept the floor, and she wore quiet house slippers she made herself. She saved her good dress and shoes for Sundays. There is a place in the back of our church just for the help; and I want her to sit by me with Papa's family, but she only sits with other help.

She told me my fainting spells had been happening since I was a babe in arms, and nobody knew why. I found myself overprotected, although seemingly uninvited in the Sarrat house.

"Amélia," I asked my mammy, "why do people talk about me when I'm right there? Don't they know I can hear?"

"Dey has no idea you be so smart. They tinks you still a baby."

"Why?" I asked.

"Cause, you is." She laughingly replied

When I was three years old, my baby bed, with the sides down and mattress set low, stood in front of the mantle, which had once been a huge fireplace; now sealed over with a fancy copper shield because a central furnace kept us warm now.

Tomas and Uncle Donald came with some tools one day and took my bed apart. They removed the sides, and lowered the mattress to the floor, with me on it. Uncle Donald ordered me to get off, but I refused.

"Non, Non, Non!" I cried and clung to the tight pink sheet adorned with baby ducks and bunnies. Uncle Donald picked me up, kicking and screaming, and slapped my behind, handing me to Amélia. I hid my face, sobbing, in her big squishy bosom as she took me away for my bath. When we returned my baby bed was gone, and a new little single bed stood in its place, Raggedy Ann was on my pillow, waiting for me.

Nannan, Aunts Cyril, Lucy, and Elise, the youngest, plus me and Amélia occupied the top floor on the Sarrat side of the house. My Leaumont cousins lived on the other side; some of them ate at our dining table with the adults.

Amélia's room was next to mine. She had her own stairwell that lead down to the kitchen and a back porch where she went through a little door to the servants' bathroom. I was not allowed to go in there.

I shared a bathroom with Aunt Cyril. We had fresh towels every day. From our veranda, I could stand on tippy toes and look out on the backyard far below. A large birdhouse sat atop a pole so high I could see purple martins in the little holes. They made a terrible racket, but uncle Gene said they were good birds because they ate mosquitos.

Amélia took care of all the girls, picking up behind us and making our beds. When the aunts dressed me up in their dolls' clothes, she scolded them. She bathed me, rocked me and sang to me. She sat up all night by my bed when I was sick. I felt bound to her by a mystical and tender love.

Amélia said she had been with the family under her maman's skirts, until she was old enough to fetch and clean. Eventually, because of her sweet nature and patience, she was taught to care for the babies and young children. She never learned to speak English but cussed proficiently in French. My uncles, so I'm told, imitated her in their frustration when they were boys, but never revealed their source and took the switch silently.

Amélia told me the story about how, in 1795, Père's ancestors had too much help and allowed a number of slaves to buy their freedom. After manumission, her great-grandfather was offered his freedom, but chose to stay with the Sarrats and was paid twenty-five cents a day for his service and each of his 10 children, beginning in 1902. Most of them were gone now.

Amélia and one niece were the last survivors of her family; sometimes she wept when she told me this story. She grew too old to do much housework, but remained with the family, having been in service all her life.

By the time I was four I began to understand that all the aunts were my mother's sisters, and Mère told me my mother was a bad girl who ran off. I didn't know where "off" was, but it didn't matter. Amélia was my mother.

I sucked my thumb, which made everyone unhappy. Mère put nasty tasting medicine on it, so I sucked the other thumb. They put socks on my hands, which I bit through, then a brace which made me cry, because it hurt, and I couldn't get my thumb in my mouth.

"Suga, you mustn't suck your thumb, your teeth will stick out," the aunts said. So reasoning that my thumb was the issue, I sucked other fingers or my toes.

From a very early age I was taught polite response and 'thank-you', and that I must be 'dainty'. The aunts read to me, showed me letters and numbers, and pictures in the little books, and we looked at a big round globe that was the whole world. Aunt Lucy gave me a little book of blank pages and encouraged me to draw pictures with colored pencils.

Sometimes I drew people; Mère asked about the picture of a princess in a pink dress. When I said, "C'est ma mama!" She frowned and made a strange moue with her mouth. "Something about you is not right, little girl," she said.

On Saturdays, my aunts and I rode bikes to a pond they called a 'lagoon' in City Park. I rode my little bike I got for Christmas, staying close to my aunts. We fed stale bread to the ducks. Other children also came to feed the ducks, some with their mothers, unless a black nursemaid accompanied them. Amélia never came to the park; she didn't have a bike.

I realized that I didn't look like the others in the family. All of them had dark, curly hair, while mine was yellow and straight; cut like the Dutch boy on the Buster Brown shoe box.

Despite the coddling and attention, I was often confronted by the aunts with hateful comments about my "bad mother". Where had she gone? Did they think I was bad, too?

I began to sneak behind heavy drapes or hide under furniture so that I could eavesdrop. My favorite hiding place was behind a large banister on the wide step at the top of the second floor. I could lay flat, making myself very small, on the dark red carpet which flowed like a river from room to room, then trickled down the stairs. I could see and hear what took place in the parlor below, but no one could see me.

A mysterious scene occurred one day when two people, a fat woman with black curly hair and a tall blonde man, came and asked Mère for me, saying I was their little girl! Mère called the woman, 'Germaine' and shouted, "You will be the death of me!"

Mère then screamed at the tall man, "You took my daughter and I'm keeping yours! You cannot support her! She will become trash like you! Leave immediately! You would not have come here if Père were at home! Get out and don't come back, you cannot have her! Look what you're doing to me, you'll give me a heart attack!"

She fanned her face with a handkerchief and sat down holding her breast. Her heart attack was miraculously over as soon as they left.

I was so frightened and confused by the event that I scurried to hide under a bed in the nearest room. Why did those people want me to go with them? Where did they want to take me? Later, I heard the grown-ups say that the man they called 'Bruce' was going away to World War II. Was the black-haired woman going, too? Was I safe?

At some point Germaine made peace with my grandparents, and returned, without Bruce, on special holidays. That winter, she brought a 3-year old boy with her and told me he was my little brother, Julius Bruce, Jr., and she called him 'Jerry'. The boy was fat, with beads of dirt around his neck which he called his 'necklaces'. When he reached out to hug me, I backed away and Germaine called me 'Prissy". That became her nickname for me. She said that I was to call her 'mother'. I attempted to repeat it, but it came out 'muzzer' because two of my front teeth were missing. I repeated "muz," and ran to hide in Amélia's skirt.

When she and Jerry visited for Easter, I welcomed him because his neck was clean. We even posed for a picture with my bike. All of the help was busy, so he and I were told to play in the back yard, while Germaine joined the grown-ups for pre-dinner cocktails. We squeezed into the dark garage where the carriages and horses used to be kept to look at the big car. In the garage, Jerry spied cans of paint amongst the tools. "Let's paint the car," he said, "You hold the can." Smearing a paint-filled brush up and down he soon had my my hands and dress covered with the same blue paint as the fender of the car.

When we were discovered, the uncles laughed, and Père gave Jerry a quarter for painting his car. Germaine took him home and I was sent to bed with no dinner. Amélia, of course, saw that I didn't go hungry by smuggling cookies to me in her pocket.

On Christmas day 'Muz' and Jerry came to pick me up in an old faded car with no top. Covered with a blanket, we clung to each other, frightened and cold in the rumble seat. She said she was taking us to visit our other grandparents, the Moores, who lived very far away.

When we arrived, everyone wanted to pick me up. Grandfather Moore, who had yellow hair like mine, squeezed me and rubbed his whiskers on my face. He asked me to count to twenty, then count by twos, which I did. He was very impressed. I have a vivid memory of him drinking wine from a fish bowl. Could that be right?

In the afternoon, the family sat very still for a photographer. The grown-ups were Bruce's brother and sisters, Auntie Hazel, Auntie Rosie, Uncle Skipper, who was also called 'Toby, Junior,' Auntie Helen and Auntie Baby. She was two years younger than Bruce, and her real name was Grace. She was named after a famous opera singer and movie star, Grace Moore. The use of the word "Auntie" was new to me, but Grandmother Moore said that was what I was to call my aunts.

I liked Auntie Rosie the best. She held me on her lap and told me she was Bruce's big sister. She whispered secrets and let me nap on her pink bed. There was only one other child there, a cousin called 'Butch' who was a few months older than me. He was blonde with blue eyes, like me, but was prettier, with curly eyelashes and curly hair. We all played together, but Butch and I couldn't run as fast or swing as high as Jerry.

After dinner, Grandfather Moore sat on a piano bench and played loud music until the piano moved and everything bounced off the top. Grandmother Moore clapped her hands and laughed along with the rest of us.

Every Christmas that they came for me, I had to leave all that Santa had brought for me at the Sarrats and go with them. There were no other children; just the three of us for many years. Bruce and Germaine would return me, along with my gifts from the Moores, but he never came inside. And then they would leave without me. I can remember standing on a hassock, looking out the big window watching them go. *She must not really be my mother; she has a boy, so I guess she doesn't need a skinny little girl.*

I well remember meeting Mère's bridge ladies when they came to our house. In preparation for their arrival she reminded me to curtsy and taught me how to pass a tray of Petite Madeleines while they played. They would arrive in carriages and fancy cars with drivers who waited outside or in the kitchen. The really old ladies smelled like rotten lace and they wanted to pinch my cheeks. They all wore glasses, had blue hair and wore dead foxes on their shoulders.

Amélia dressed me in ruffles, like a lampshade. My hair was shiny but straight. As I passed the Madeleines the ladies laughed about how thin and pale I was. *Do they think I'm deaf?* One of the ladies asked, "Mignon, what are you going to do about that poor child?"

"I have a new tonic," Mère replied, "She's not growing like she should."

Another lady commented, "I've heard that unwanted children never do."

I was shocked. *Am I a poor child? I know I'm thin, but poor? Am I really unwanted?* I put down the tray and slipped out. They didn't miss me.

Mère spent many afternoons entertaining friends. While ladies visited in her parlor to gossip, she would give me a piece of white material stretched between two wooden circles. "Here, child, take this and draw pictures on the fabric with this needle and embroidery thread." Everything I tried was a pitiful mess, until the day Mère showed me some special stitches. She insisted the backside must look as neat as the front. That was so hard!

I liked to draw pictures on paper, and I discovered that if I drew flowers or puppies or houses on the taut white material, I could follow the lines of what I drew. I hid it from her until I learned to do it right. I wanted very much to please Mère.

On the days she sewed, I watched closely as fabric was laid out and cut for trousseau dresses for two of my aunts who had received diamond engagement rings.

"What is a 'true sew?" I asked. Mère said, "a trousseau is what a bride wears, when she takes off her wedding dress."

"Doesn't she have pajamas?" I asked innocently.

Mère showed me how to put little round weights on the tissue paper pattern and how to place pieces carefully on the fabric so no material was wasted. When she finished, I was to fold the pattern along the exact same creases, so it would fit back in the envelope and she could use it over and over. They each cost twenty-five cents! Most of the scraps were mine to make my dolly's clothes by hand; I wasn't allowed to use the Singer.

When she sewed at her machine, Tomas moved it away from the wall, and I could stand on a box behind it to raise and lower the presser foot whenever she told me. I loved that and soon I guessed just when to do it!

When Auntie Helen had her wedding in the back yard at the Moore's house, I was her flower girl. I had a blue fluffy feather in my hair and wore a pretty blue dress. In the garden, I walked on a make-believe aisle of plain white fabric that covered the grass in a straight line. Their house was enormous, and the reception was held there at night, but I didn't see that part.

Nannan Hilda was the first Sarrat aunt to be married. I was her flower girl when I was six. This time I wore a long pink dress and carried a little basket down the middle of the long aisle of the church. I sprinkled flower petals on the white cloth all the way to the altar. The reception for 500 guests was held in Père's house. All the downstairs furniture was stowed in trucks for the event and brought back the next day.

Once more I had a role in a wedding when Aunt Cyril got married and I was so proud because I already knew what to do.

Uncle Donald went to work in Memphis and came home married to a tall lady named “Polly”. She had no job, so Mère made her take me to dance class and sit there while eight little girls fumbled and tapped at Miss Laurent's School. Aunt Polly didn't talk much, so I had no clue that she didn't like this ‘job’. I suspect that's why she was always angry with me.

Mère always sat at one end of the dining table. There was a button under the carpet at her feet so that she could buzz servers to bring food, dessert, or clear the table. When the room was dark in the daytime and nobody was watching, I would crawl under the table and press the button with my hand. Mary, the cook, always got upset and chased me away. She didn't have a broom like Amélia, so she swatted me with a dishrag.

Not included in that coterie, I was fed earlier, in a breakfast room off the kitchen with some of the help. They had their own dishes and glasses, explaining that white folk didn't like to eat off plates used by black folks. I was confused. because I loved Amélia so much I would let her drink from my Shirley Temple cup any day. At mealtimes, I was dressed up and was careful not to soil my clothes, unless I was served something I didn't like, which I hid in my pockets. Amélia scolded me when she found it. And she always found it. The vegetable soup presented a problem. I tried once, but I soon learned not to put soup in my pocket.

At the age of 6, Amélia explained that I was getting to be a big girl and would have to learn to speak English in preparation for starting school. The aunts helped me practice upstairs where Papa couldn't hear, because he only allowed us to speak French in the house.

I tried on my school uniform which consisted of a white blouse with a navy-blue skirt that buttoned onto it. A little blue beanie went on my head and a dark blue triangle of silk was tied around my neck. I loved the way I looked in the mirror. My satchel was prepared with pencils, crayons, a tablet, and my lunch (half a sandwich and a cookie, each wrapped in cheese cloth). Aunt Lucy taught me to write my letters, and I printed 'LYNNE MOORE', on my red Big Chief tablet. I practiced eating lunch on the patio by myself, though I knew the help watched through the windows.

Suga practicing school lunch

On the first day of school, Amélia took my hand and we walked along the bayou to the school yard where she turned me over to a nun. To me she was a lady dressed like a saint.

I watched, amazed, while the other children cried and threw tantrums when they kissed their mothers goodbye. Taking the hand of one girl bigger than myself, I tried to comfort her. “Don’t cry,” I said, “this will be fun.” But she didn’t stop crying and watched sadly while her mother left the yard. “My name is Lynne, I told her”, and she whispered, “My name is Elaine.”

Sister Lucille led the class though an old building and up a staircase with wide dark brown steps, worn down in the middle. Ushering us into a classroom, she showed us our desks. Being short, I was told to sit in the front row; bigger kids sat in the back. From the first day, the nuns spoke lovingly about Jesus and the Blessed Mother. Sister Lucille said Mary would be our Jiminy Cricket, sitting on our shoulders to guide and help us. I never forgot that. We ate lunch at our desks that first day; then each day after that we went downstairs to eat in the basement at little low tables. After lunch we had a few minutes to go outside and take big breaths of fresh air and walk around in front of the priests’ house or look through the fence at Bayou St. John.

When three o’clock came, we were told to stand in line. Sister called them ‘ranks’, and we put a finger to our lips, which meant no talking. She led us out to where the mothers waited in the yard. Amélia stood far off to the side, and I suspected she had been there all day. She hugged me before we walked home. I couldn’t wait to tell her all the events of the day.

“Sister taught us to write numbers and clapped when we counted! There are pictures of elves above the blackboards, all around the room, each bending in the shape of a letter. My favorite is ‘S’, but I can draw others. I waited for the class to learn things I already knew, so Sister let me help a little girl who didn’t know much. That is the only time we talked in school. The best thing is that we can go back every day! Je suis excite!”

One morning, a few weeks later, when I was grim instead of smiling, Sister Lucille bent down and put her arm around me. asking, “What’s wrong, Lynne? You look so sad.”

“Mère is very angry with me, Sister; when the help does anything wrong, she sends them away. I er, I wet my bed,”

I whispered. “Please, Sister, if she sends me away, please ask her to give me to you.”

The bombing in Europe showed up in the newsreels at the theater and it was scary. I wondered if wars ever came to us? I hoped not. I learned about ration stamps. The aunts couldn’t have nylon stockings and the tires on the car had to last a long time because rubber was very precious. Mère was able to get butter and sugar by holding all the stamps for the servants along with ours.

My uncles began appearing in uniform. Uncle Skeeter (Norman) was like a big brother to me, because he was only fourteen years older. He flew in a plane that was shot down, and he was captured by the Germans. I wrote him letters and Mère sent packages to a place called Stalag Luft 3. Neighbors came over for a “block rosary” on Monday nights. We all knelt on the carpet in the main parlor and prayed for all of the men to be kept safe.

After sixteen months, a friend called to say that she had overheard a shortwave broadcast giving the names of prisoners who had been liberated and Uncle Skeeter was among them. We then learned that Uncle Warren, Aunt Cyril’s husband, was there to free the prisoners at Uncle Skeeter’s prison camp. Everyone cried a lot and I held Amélia’s hand while she cried, too. Skeeter returned but was never the same; soon he got polio and was crippled for the rest of his life. Mère blamed the ‘damn Nazis’.

I was afraid I wouldn’t live to grow up, since the war was still out there.

For as long as I can remember, Aunt Lucy took me to the movies on Saturdays. She let me sit on the arm of her seat so I could see between the people in front of us. My nose kept running one day, and Lucy told me to wipe it with my dress because she didn’t have a hanky. When we got into the light in front of the popcorn and candy counter, my dress was covered with blood! I was afraid I was in trouble for spoiling my pretty blue dress. That week, Tomas drove me to a hospital where my tonsils were removed, and I ate sherbet twice each day. He came back to take me home two days later, and no one ever mentioned the ruined dress.

Chapter 4

Germaine told us that Bruce had permission for his family to join him at Ft. Eustis in Virginia. "Priss," she said, using that hated name, "we're going to live in Virginia where Dad's Army base is. He wanted me to ask if you would like to come with us?" In my child's mind, I quickly concluded that if the Army, was in Virginia then that place would be dangerous. There must be a war there; I was horrified.

Also, I really didn't know them very well. I knew my Sarrat family better than I knew Germaine and Jerry, and I didn't know Bruce at all! Unknown things frightened me. I suspected Germ didn't really want me, anyway, and she confirmed it, saying, "If you don't want to come it'll be okay. I'll have Jerry write you letters. It'll be fun to get mail!"

I was going into fourth grade when she came to say goodbye. Germaine and Mère argued and said ugly things. I heard her shout my name before she left.

That night I was put to bed with a headache so severe I cried out, "Make it stop! Please, Amelià, make it stop!" I threw up on the bedspread. Amélia wiped my face, her own tears running down her cheeks. She took the spread off the bed, then gave me crushed ice and Coke to sip. Amelià sang me to sleep with my favorite lullaby, Frere Jacques.

Was Germaine really my mother? When I asked questions, Aunt Lucy told me the rumor that I was Auntie Rosie's child. What was I to believe? No one really wanted to talk about the past, and I was in the middle, with no real answers. The headaches came more often and lasted longer than ever.

When I didn't have migraines, my classmates and I went out to the movies; Tomas drove and picked them up. He paid for my movie ticket, waited, then brought us home. Any time we passed a house that was boarded up I tried to remember where it was, so if Mère ever sent me away, I would have a place to go; a shelter from the cold and rain.

My friends spoke about their families and how much they had to help around the house because they didn't have servants. When I spoke about Amélia and Tomas, the girls giggled behind their hands and made funny eyes at each other because they didn't live that way. I pretended not to notice. They loved driving around in the big black car driven by a chauffeur, which I'm sure is the only reason they included me.

At twelve I made my confirmation in a lovely white dress and veil, much like first communion. That meant it was time to put my childhood behind, though I didn't feel grown up. Amélia still dressed me up at 5 o'clock each day and fussed over my long blonde hair but now I had to eat dinner with the adults. Having to sit on a phone book <u>and</u> a pillow to reach the table. Never hungry, I still put food in my pockets.

I sat on Mère's left, but she was so busy holding court she didn't pay attention to me except to say, "Eat, Lynne." When I was little they said that so often, I thought 'Eat Lynne' was my name. Now they mostly called me, "Suga," except for Mère who refused to say it.

When I had eaten in the breakfast room, I had watched as Mary pushed through the swinging door with her hip into the dining room. Now I saw how she strained on the other side of that door to carry huge platters. She placed them on silver trivets in front of Mère, who filled and then passed each plate. I noticed that the adult voices stopped on half a word when they saw Mary, so as not to share family business with the help.

My aunts would talk when they thought I couldn't hear them, amazed over things I drew. "She sees things nobody else sees", they would say. Then I remembered Mère saying I was not 'right.' But I was a good student, always proud to show my report card to the uncles and aunts. Plus, I got a quarter from each of the uncles for every 'A'. That was a lot of loot for my bank, because they were all 'A's'.

"Don't hide your light under a bushel", is what the sisters advised me. They had taken an interest in me, encouraging me to take college prep electives instead of homemaking courses. They seemed to know my grandparents had taken me in, and were extra kind and considerate, letting me perform in plays, and make announcements at assemblies. I wanted to excel in school to prove I wasn't like Germaine, who, I had been told, spent her schooldays causing mayhem.

In October of 1948, I got the word that Germaine had another baby, a little boy named Tommy.

That same year Aunt Cyril and Uncle Warren had a sweet baby girl they named Betty Ann. She was chubby and had blonde ringlets all over her head. I was not allowed to pick her up but played with her all the time. I pretended Betty was my baby sister and told her stories, and promised that when I grew up, she could be the flower girl at my wedding.

They slept in the room next to mine. I listened closely when Aunt Cyril and Uncle Warren went into the bathroom at night; since I knew nothing about sex, I assumed that's where they "did it", whatever "it" was. My friends didn't know either, but they were also curious, and we imagined ridiculous things.

The single aunts and I sometimes stayed up after Mère made her nightly expedition in and out of rooms, up and down hallways. She was looking for scissors. We all sewed, so there were many pairs of scissors in our rooms. When Mère saw a pair on a desk or table, she covered them up with a scarf, a magazine, a book, whatever she could find.

"Girls," she warned, "you must not leave scissors out in the open! If they get in, they'll use them to kill you." Her mission completed, she went downstairs to bed.

"Who are "they?" I asked in a whisper.

Aunt Lucy offered, "You know, 'they' are bad guys who sneak into houses and 'get' people."

"Get them to do what?" I asked.

"You don't have to worry, Suga, we're on the third floor. Nobody is going to sneak up here. It's all because when she was a girl someone broke into their house and her father shot him."

"And did he stab anyone with scissors?" I was intrigued.

"No," replied Aunt Lucy, "Her mother had put all the scissors out of sight."

Once a year, after I turned fourteen, Mère took me to her doctor for an examination. As usual, we didn't leave the house to go downtown without our white gloves and hats. Dr. Charbonnet's nurse took off my hat and gloves and panties, handed them to me, then helped me climb up to lay on a cold table. The doctor felt my flat breasts, then he examined me with his finger between my legs, hurting me. He shook his head and turning to Mère, he said, "No, nothing wrong, she's just immature." And then speaking to me, "You can get dressed now, little girl."

They never explained what this was all about, and I was too upset to ask, wiping tears from my eyes with my panties before I put them back on. Afterwards, Mère would take me out for a soda and then buy me a sweater or a hat. Surely, no one in the house was going to teach me about sex, or even about menstruation, so I learned everything from girls at school and the nuns.

"The Emperor Napoleon was invited to come to New Orleans when he was exiled to Elba, but he died in 1821 before he got here. This building was prepared for him, but he never saw it." Père told me as we sipped tea in the Napoleon House on Chartres Street in the French Quarter. My grandparents were taking me to see historical places and teaching me about our culture. They also took me to the opera and the ballet when it came to New Orleans.

"Please tell me, Mère", I inquired, "was Père a good catch?"

"My dear, we never would have thought of such a thing! But he was very handsome. My sister, Marie Haydee, was courted by Uncle George, and I was the chaperone; they could never be left alone for the two years of courtship. Because I was only fourteen, Père's maman insisted he go along to keep me company. Père asked me to marry him on my sixteenth birthday. I was delighted and, of course, he had the approval of my Papa. Mardi Gras season was beginning, and I was to be a maid in the Olympian's ball and would have made my debut shortly thereafter. Of course, being presented to society meant nothing, since we were already engaged."

"Was she a beautiful bride, Père?" I asked. Before he could answer, Mère interrupted in a severe voice. "Who is 'she', the cat's mother? You must never speak of your elders in their presence as 'she' or 'he'!"

"Yes, darling girl, she took my breath away." Père flattered me, "and you are just as beautiful, but with fair hair."

Mère went on, "My sisters made my lace veil by hand in only six months, with some assistance from my mother and the help. After our wedding, they began a christening dress for the babies they thought I would have. You wore it and your children will also."

As part of our education, Tomas took the aunts, me and Mère to the cemeteries, often referred to as "cities of the dead". We read the names on the big stone tombs and she Mère told about some of the people she had known who were buried there.

"Why are the graves in stone houses, Mère?" I was curious.

"There has never been a time that the ground under New Orleans was solid. The early coffins popped up right out of the ground before they learned to enclose them in stone. The water table is very high; just a few feet down and the grave becomes soggy, filling with water. The caskets would literally float." This was serious but amusing.

I remember when Mère had Tomas take us to Baton Rouge and made us spit on Governor Huey P. Long's grave, on the Governor's birthday. I had no choice and I was never told why. In later years, I made myself unavailable to go on that outing.

Mère also told funny stories of her life as a girl. She and her sisters once had a spitting contest and she spit herself right off a third story balcony into a tree. A butler had to climb the tree to get her down. Mère's life was pure haute monde, and she got very animated when she told of her youth. I loved to see her like that.

Mère's father, Victor Michel, had built two grand houses, one in the Garden District in New Orleans, and the other in Mississippi. They must have been rich, because they had a beach house, where the family escaped the heat of the city in summer. Women, children and the help remained in the beach house while the men rode a train into the city to conduct business each day.

Once, little Mignon accompanied a driver in a carriage to meet her father at the train station. She insisted on sitting on the little rear step where a footman would stand. She bounced off onto a dirt road and the driver didn't even know she was gone. When he came back from the station with her father, she was found sitting in the dust and sand in the middle of the road.

The summer house was destroyed by a hurricane in 1917; they rebuilt it, but it was destroyed again the following September.

After Bruce's three-year tour in Virginia, he was reassigned to Manila, unaccompanied, so Germ brought Jerry and Tommy back to New Orleans. Taking a job with Motion Picture Advertising, she had arranged for Jerry and me to act in commercials. The first time, we held hands in the back of the car, both a little frightened, but we met nice people who took us to places, sometimes to a film studio, or a park, or on city streets. They told us what to say and when to say it; mostly it was just lots of lights and cameras and waiting, waiting, waiting for the director to say, "Roll."

Besides AFTRA and SAG union cards, we got Social Security cards because we made money, but after a while this got boring and I was glad when Germ left that job. I didn't know I would use those cards when I needed a job many years later.

When it was time to join Bruce in Manila, he again demanded that she take me away from the Sarrats and bring me with the two boys to live there. Jerry told me about the fights they had over me. Once again, she asked me, casually, if I would like to go along. Such a dilemma she thrust on me! I was already registered for high school with all my friends, and the only one to help me make this decision was Mère, who said, "Your father will make you sleep with your brothers, you're better off here. He will put you to work to support him."

The Sarrat house seemed empty. Everyone else had been married, even Elise and Norman now had homes of their own. Remaining with Mère, Papa, and Aunt Lucy, I continued to faint and have migraine headaches and missed a lot of school, but never fell behind.

Tommy, Suga, Jerry, and Germaine
Spring 1956, New Orleans

Chapter 5

A lineup of nuns greeted us in 1950 as the freshmen entered the impressive portal of St. Joseph Academy. As I passed the last of the sisters there to greet us, one of them took my arm and said, “We knew your mother, Miss Moore, we are going to watch you VERY carefully.” I wasn’t worried because I was a good girl.

Finding a date for the first sock hop of the year seemed futile in an all girls’ school, as I had no boyfriend. My friend, Andy, from grammar school, went to a seminary to study to become a priest, so I couldn’t invite him. Fortunately, a classmate arranged a blind date for me with a shy boy named Rodney.

One of my more mature and confident classmates showed up with a boy who caught my eye. Jim was tan and well dressed, with brown curly hair. I hoped he would ask me to dance but he didn’t even know I was there. Although, I don’t know how he could have missed me, Aunt Elise had talked me into wearing a pink ruffled dress and a braid down my back. All the other girls looked polished and glamorous in circular skirts, Peter Pan collars, and current hairdos.

Months later, as Sadie Hawkins Day approached, the girls decided to mix things up by swapping beaus. They each put their boyfriend's name in a hat and drew out a different one to invite to the backwards party. I froze when I realized whose name I had drawn! That night, phoning Jim to extend the invitation took courage. I expected him to say 'no'.

He answered the phone. "Hi, Jim, this is Lynne." I began.

"Who?" he asked.

"Lynne Moore, I'm in Liz's class at the Academy." I replied.

"Do I know you?" He asked cautiously.

"We met at the Freshman Sock Hop in September. I'm calling to ask you to a Sadie Hawkins dance next Friday night as my date. We have to invite the boys." Was I talking too fast? I was so nervous.

"No, I'm sorry. I'm dating Liz; she wouldn't agree to this."

"She knows, and she doesn't mind. We all put names in a hat and drew out someone different for this backwards party. Liz put your name in and I drew you." Please help me, Virgin Mary.

He was reluctant, but despite his doubts, he said yes! We double dated with his friend, Eddie, who drove his father's car. I taught Jim a new dance step and he surprised me by asking if I'd go out with him again. I was trying not to faint. There was no goodnight kiss, but he took my phone number, Audubon 1372. I had an extension phone that sat on a little table in my room. When it rang the next afternoon, I picked up on the first ring, sure the call wasn't for me. I stood at my bedroom window looking down on acres of green grass, with pencil and paper ready to take a message.

"Sarrat's residence, Lynne speaking."

Silence. Finally, "Hi, this is Jim."

"Oh, hello?" My eyes got enormous; I squeezed them shut. I drummed my fingers on the windowsill. Oh my god. He's calling me!

"Did you have a good time at the party?" he asked. I opened my eyes wide.

"I did. Thank you for being such a good sport and wearing the horrible celery and lettuce corsage." Jim said, "All the guys tried to get into the spirit. I was glad we rode with Eddie and his date so that we didn't have to wear that thing on a bus!"

"Did you want to talk to me?" I can't believe this. I nervously pulled one of the buttons off my sweater.

"Well, yeah. That dance step you taught me, where did you learn that?" he asked.

"My aunts and uncles are always dancing and teaching me." I told him.

"What I really called for, is to see if you'd go out with me again." He stated.

"Are you sure? What if Liz finds out?" I was very nervous.

"Do you have a date next Friday night?" he asked without answering my question.

"No, not really. I don't have any dates. I mean, not Friday dates. Not er... next Friday." Oh my god, I am going to faint.

"Will you go to the movies with me?" He asked.

"What?" I was stalling.

"I asked if you would let me take you to the movies." He repeated.

I took a deep breath and said, "I would love to." When I hung up I hugged myself and ran to tell Amélia.

Jim called again before our date and asked to meet my parents. "Grandparents." I corrected.

As soon as Tomas let him in on Friday, Mère and Père were alerted and when they entered the parlor, Jim stood up. I started to say, Mère and P..,"., but Jim interrupted, "Madame and M. Sarrat, let me introduce myself. I am James Edward Mouton; I'm in my second year at Jesuit High School. I was born in Lafayette; my father is a Postal Inspector and I'm sixteen years old. Oh, yes, and we're Catholic."

Mère smiled graciously, "How do you do?"

Père suppressed a chuckle and offered his hand. "James, if you were applying for a job I'd have to give it to you. I like a man who's well prepared."

"Well, sir, in a way I guess I am applying for the position of escort. It would be my pleasure to take this young lady," he looked my way, "to the movies. If you'll permit it, we can make the first show and be home by eleven. And please call me Jim." I was astonished, he was so smooth.

"Be on your way, and enjoy yourselves," Père led us to the front door and opened it himself, something I had never seen him do before.

Outside I asked, "Where's your car?" The night was crisp, and a sense of joy overwhelmed me.

"Sorry, we're going to ride the bus. I don't drive. I have epilepsy, but don't worry, I won't have a seizure or anything. I'm on medication that controls it. Do you mind a short bus ride?" He looked at me sideways.

"Of course not." He held my hand as we walked the two blocks to the bus stop. I saw another old gray house from the bus window, a boarded-up place I needed to remember. I said nothing to Jim, he would never understand that I might need a safe place to go if I were sent away.

When he bought the tickets, he paid for a child's admission for me, probably because I was so short and looked so young. He held my small hand in his sweaty one all through the movie and gave me my first peck on the cheek when he brought me home.

We fell into the habit of going out together often on Friday nights for the rest of that year.

Dashing through the hall at school, I rushed past Sister Albina, an ascetic, formidable nun who caught me by my blue sweater and said, "Miss Moore! Why are you so childish and silly? There is so much to you! You are not your mother! You need to grow up, I know you will shine! You will leave footprints on this earth!"

This was a shocker! I had never looked at myself or my behavior. All I had in my head was that nobody wanted me. "Thank you, Sister, I'm sorry. Er, thank you, Sister." She surprised and inspired me to act more mature. I walked sedately to my next class with much to think about.

On weekends most of the family, including the help, went to our summer home in Bay St. Louis, Mississippi. Jim called me every week night begging me to stay home on weekends, so I could go out with him. But that wasn't allowed until after my seventeenth birthday. He offered me his fraternity pin, regardless, asking me to go steady, which I accepted.

In the summer, we took a hayride to Abita Springs for the day, driving through a fierce rainstorm on the way home. Each couple snuggled under their large beach towels, getting soaked in the bed of the truck. Jim kissed me and held me all the way back to New Orleans. Neither of us guessed he'd ask me to return his pin when he started college.

Grandfather Toby and Grandmother Pauline Moore had turned over their house to Auntie Rosie and her husband, Uncle Al Rufin. They planned to stay there and be cared for as long as they lived. Rosie now had two children, a boy she named Jean Pierre and a little girl, Denise. The house was often filled with relatives and friends who swam, danced, and played parlor games. Much of the grand house remained dark, because they hosted everyone in a new addition with a massive picture window overlooking the pool and beautiful ancient oaks.

Subdividing the gardens behind the house, they turned the long driveway into a street ending in a cul-de-sac, then built six houses on the spacious grounds. One went to their son, Pierre, when he married.

Suga with Jim Mouton
Jesuit Jr/Sr Prom 1952

Jim and I enjoyed the New Orleans social whirl, Mardi Gras balls, fraternity and sorority parties. Mère bought as much special fabric as I needed for my formal dresses, which I designed and made myself. Jim's parents bought him a tuxedo when renting them became too costly. He looked very handsome and mature. Three years of dances, formal balls and football games passed in a flash. Many nights, double dating with friends, we parked on the lakefront and necked for hours, but we never considered giving up our virtue. We were not ready to fall from grace. When we went to functions at Jesuit High School, an elderly priest named Father Enst, whose black shirt was stained with tobacco juice and his lunch, always shadowed Jim. Seems he believed that Jim was best suited for the priesthood and he considered me a hindrance to that. Usually, as part of his goodbye, he would say, "I'm going to get him before you do."

At 3 a.m., every Sunday morning, church bells pealed in the French Quarter for a fisherman's mass conducted in St. Louis Cathedral in Jackson Square. Young people satisfied their Sunday obligation in the wake of graduations, dances, and masked balls at this early mass. Inebriated escorts reeking of beer and booze, slumbered through the mass, while disheveled young ladies remained upright, with ruined shoes askew on the marble floor. Velvet wraps, furs and jeweled handbags were tossed carelessly on the pews. But we attended mass!

Tuxedos dusted with powdered sugar were ready for the dry cleaner after eating beignets at the Café du Monde, and evening gowns had damp, stained hemlines from walking in the French Quarter. No one cared. Personal maids cleaned up all evidence of barhopping before the dresses were stored or given to the help.

When Jim was a senior at Jesuit he followed football seriously. One Saturday, he and I, along with another couple were invited for an early supper at Auntie Rosie's. We were headed to LSU stadium in Baton Rouge for a game and this was on our route.

Rosie's reaction when we arrived was totally unexpected. She had always welcomed Elaine and all my friends, but literally turned stark white when Jim introduced Charles Merriea.

"We are so pleased to meet you, young man," Grandmother Pauline said. "We once had another guest with that name some years ago."

"That would be my father," Charles offered, "I'll have to ask him if he remembers coming to your home, Mrs. Moore."

"That's silly, Mother," Rosie injected abruptly, "Don't bother your father, Charles, he would have long ago forgotten if he had been here eighteen or twenty years ago. Just forget it."

After dinner, Rosie took me aside while the young men were getting our coats, "Lynne, darling, please promise me you will never, under any circumstances, date Charles Merriea."

"I wouldn't date him, Auntie Rose, I'm wearing Jim's fraternity pin." I said.

"In the future, anything can happen. You and Jim could break up, but you are never to go with him, understand? I want your solemn word." She persisted.

"Will you tell me what this is about?" I asked.

"Just promise, please. Your friends are ready to leave. Someday we'll talk about it again."

"I promise, Auntie Rosie, if it's important to you."

"I love you, Suga. Go, have a good time and remember your promise. Trust me, it is more important than you know, he could be related to you."

It flew out of my mind like a hungry bird and I never thought of it again until I heard a revelation from Germ in New York a little over a year later

"Good morning, Mère." It was 7:30 a.m., on a Tuesday morning. I was dressing for school while Mère poked around, fingering things on my dresser and desk, lifting papers or scarves as though she were looking for something I might be hiding. The aunts laughed about it when she did the same in their rooms, and though they resented it, no one would dare say so to their mother. "Good morning, Mère," I repeated.

"Did Aunt Lucy say anything to you, Lynne, about going away?" she asked.

"No, Mère. Away, where?" I questioned.

"She failed to come home from work, didn't call, and didn't come in all night. Do you know where she can be?" Mere seemed desperate.

"Did you call her office?" I suggested.

Mère moved to the window where the early light shone off the diamonds in her ears, at her wrist and bosom. *Why does she wear all that before eight o'clock in the morning? Does she sleep in them?*

"Père is calling right now; we're very concerned." She smoothed my pillow and attempted to pull the spread up on my bed. A good fairy named Amélia kept my room looking perfect. I never did it.

"Excuse me, Mère, I have to go to school." I edged past her and headed down the stairs, assuming she was overreacting.

When I got home at four that afternoon, all the lights were on. Ordinarily, I came home to darkness downstairs, with just the help in the kitchen. Heavy drapes were normally closed to keep the sun from fading the upholstery. The house was full of aunts, uncles, and cousins, all milling about, whispering. Mère held a lacy handkerchief to her eyes and was sobbing. Most shocking of all was the sight of Père sitting by the telephone with his head in his hands.

Uncle Gene, Hilda's husband, was standing nearest the door, and I stepped up behind him and asked quietly, "What's happening?"

Gene was not much taller than my five-foot-two, a sweet little man with a round face and a receding hairline. He whispered to me, "The police have been called, Lucy has disappeared."

"Disappeared? You think she's been kidnapped?" I asked.

"We don't know what to think." He replied.

I went to Mère, knelt in front of her chair and took her hands in mine. "Lynne, do you know any of her friends?" She asked, "Did she ever mention a man to you?"

"No. Whenever she went anywhere she usually took me along, but no one else. Mère, she'll come home, please don't imagine the worst." I pleaded.

Bossy Uncle Donald asked, in a voice that gave me chills, "Lynne, do you know how she paid for the piano she bought for you?"

"I would have to guess she paid for it out of her salary. She never said a word about how much it cost. Why?" I didn't understand what this had to do with her disappearance.

"She spent a lot of money on you." His tone was accusative.

"I guess she did, but she always seemed to have money. What are you thinking, that I had something to do with her disappearance?" I was incredulous.

"The music store where she bought it, called. She fell behind on payments; they want the piano back and interest is accumulating every week." He answered.

"Oh, no!" I was stunned. She bought the beautiful mahogany spinet that I had been asking for since I was a little girl. The store offered a year of lessons with the purchase and I had taken advantage for the last six months; having Tomas drive me downtown to Werline's on Canal Street. He waited an hour while I learned scales and simple songs, which I practiced religiously at home.

Père spoke up then, "You go on upstairs and attend to your lessons, cherie, and get dressed for dinner."

I was happy to get away and did as Père said. I loved and respected him and always felt sorry when Mère berated him in front of everyone. He was too refined to retaliate.

Dinner that night was funereal. Mère cried constantly. After their demitasse and brandy, the adults assembled in the largest parlor and I went upstairs to finish my homework.

For once, Père didn't have on his burgundy satin smoking jacket he usually wore after he came home from work. Had he even gone to work with one of his beloved daughters missing?

Next morning, The Times Picayune carried Lucy's picture and an article about her disappearance. I came down for breakfast, dressed for school, but was ordered to take off my uniform. I was told I wouldn't be going to school; I hated to miss a day, hoping for a scholarship for college.

Long after dark I heard a commotion and though I was too big to recline on the top step and eavesdropped, I sat there in the dark and listened. What I learned was that Lucy had left a note saying she could be reached through General Delivery in Mobile. Four uncles had driven to Mobile and waited at the post office until Lucy came to check for her mail. They took her by both arms and forced her into their car, fighting.

She confessed that the loan payments for the piano had gotten out of hand; she couldn't catch up and thought if she ran away they'd have to forgive the debt. Even I knew better than that. They hustled her upstairs after a quick bowl of gumbo and locked her in her room. At that point, Mère stopped crying and reigned supreme once again.

The following day when I came down, Mère sat alone at the breakfast table.

"Good morning, Mère." I said.

She sternly addressed me as I sat down. "It is not a good morning for your Aunt Lucy. Do you know what you've caused?"

"I caused?" I was stunned.

"You've caused your dear aunt, who has loved and indulged you all these years to lose her mind!" she accused.

"What did I do?" Intimidated, I fought back tears.

"It was you who wanted a piano she couldn't afford! Instead of going to Père, she took out a loan with high interest that frightened her so badly she walked out on her job and ran away." Mère replied stiffly.

"Mère, please, I would never have put her in jeopardy if she had ever mentioned to me that she couldn't handle it. I just assumed..." I said plaintively.

"You're just like your mother, little girl, selfish and headstrong. Everything is, me, me, me; not caring a whit about anyone else! I should never have taken you in." She snapped

"But, Mère, no, please, I..." I begged.

“Please, nothing. Go upstairs and get dressed, you’re going to school today. I want you out of my sight!” she commanded.

As I went through my day, I couldn’t help but compare Mère to Grandmother Pauline. Occasionally, Tomas drove me to visit her in Jefferson parish where she lived with Auntie Rosie. I was fascinated by her graceful, manicured hands, fragrant with Jergens almond-scented lotion. When she drove her own car, she wore gloves to protect those beautiful hands. She maintained a majestic mien, even in her coke-bottle-thick bifocals.

But it was her goodness that most impressed me. If she ever heard anyone speaking of another’s shortcomings, her immediate reaction was to interject a positive thought, and suggest they seek out the good in everyone. Her home was usually filled with vases of fresh flowers and the delicious smell of a steamboat round of beef in the oven. I had the impression Pauline’s goal in life was to make everyone happy. She was a role model for me at seventeen.

After a long respite of many weeks, Lucy recovered and got another job. Père convinced Werline’s to cancel the interest and he paid off the loan. Nothing more was ever said about it.

In 1953, the Arrow Room was a ballroom on the Airline Highway. The orchestra was tuning up when Jim and I joined our friends at a long table on one side of the massive room. I had made my sky-blue tulle-over-taffeta gown, and Aunt Lucy had carefully covered my shoes in matching fabric. Jim was in his white dinner jacket with Bermuda shorts, a fad that had sprung up all over town. The first song, “At Last”, was appropriate, because we had counted the days until that last big dance of the season. Our childhood was slipping away.

Jim’s arm went around me before we took the first step out onto the dance floor. It should have been like so many other dances, but this night was strange for me. For over three years we had professed our love, even drew up a five-year plan to marry after college. But that night, I had an inkling that something was not right, and for the first time I didn't feel confident in Jim, as though he was keeping a secret. Leaving the dance earlier than usual, he had very little to say on the way home, seeming to be concentrating on his driving. He barely kissed me goodnight.

Remembering how thrilled I had been when I received my own front door key, I placed it in the key hole as Jim quietly stepped back and left. Once inside the heavily decorated glass door, I unhooked my hoopskirt and crinoline and silently dropped them, stepping out once they hit the floor, confident that Amélia would retrieve them before the household woke up. Silently, I tiptoed up the stairs carrying my shoes, careful to avoid the eighth stair that squeaked.

It was Friday, a week later, when he called for me for the Jesuit Homecoming Game at City Park stadium; close enough to walk on a nice night. He normally held my hand when we went anywhere, but that night he didn't. The moon was just over the bayou, and I felt strangely apprehensive. Breaking my reverie, Jim finally spoke. "I went with George Saltzman for orientation yesterday at Loyola."

"Are you excited about starting college?" I asked, wrapping my arms tightly around myself.

"Yes, but there are other things on my mind." He and George had been friends since they were kids, so I was surprised and had to ask, "What things? Did you have a falling-out with George?"

"Good old George, nobody falls out with him. No, but we made a pact and you're not going to like it."

"A pact?" We had crossed the wooden bridge over Bayou St. John when he stopped under the streetlight at the far side. He took both my hands in his. My pulse began to race; something was wrong.

"It's about girls." He said.

"What girls? Anyone I know?" My heart had stopped.

"We agreed... er, that since we will be college men, we won't date any girl more than once during our freshman year."

"No one girl twice in a year, not even me? Are you asking for your fraternity pin back? Is that what you're telling me? Are we breaking up? What about our plans?" I was in shock.

"It's just for a year." He cajoled.

I was crushed. I was going to have one date with him in a year? And he was going to date other girls. I had been elected president of my student council and would have no escort for my big year.

The pin was symbolic. Unpinning it from my blouse, I held it out in my open hand and held my breath. He would have to take it, if that's what he wanted. I was not going to hand it to him.

He didn't say anything; just looked at the ground, avoiding my eyes.

"Fine." I said, finally, in the stifling silence. Did I want somebody who didn't want me? I had that kind of existence at home, but never expected this from my Jim. He took the pin out of my hand and put it in his pocket, still not meeting my eyes. I was shaking inside. When I found my voice I asked, "Would it be a violation of your agreement for a college man to walk his ex-fiancée home?" He didn't respond, we walked back over the bridge in silence.

He turned and left me at my door without a word. Was he angry? Embarrassed? What? I was certainly not going to beg.

That night, when the aunts gathered for our usual late tête-à-tête, on the balcony after dinner, I didn't mention what had happened. They loved him and would have taken his side.

Chapter 6

I knew that at the end of the school year, I'd have to do something if I hadn't won a college scholarship. I seemed to have a gift with a pencil, so I thought of commercial art. I had approached Père about attending a fine arts school in the French Quarter, but he was not pleased.

"Absolutely not!" He declared. "Refined young ladies don't do that, and certainly not in the Vieux Carrè! That's a den of iniquity!"

"What do refined young ladies do, Papa?" I demanded.

"They get married and have babies. Mère and I are waiting for you to marry so we can close up this mausoleum and retire to Bay St. Louis." He stated frankly.

Early in September, of 1953, a timid little freshman approached the dining table at the Academy where officers of the student council, prefect of the sodality, editor of our school paper, and captains of various teams all congregated for lunch. She distracted us, stepping up on my right and introducing herself as Joan Lake. Speaking in a low voice, only to me, she asked if I knew her brother, Freddie.

"Yes, I think I remember meeting him at a Jesuit function, why? You know you are interrupting a meeting, Joan." The other girls stopped talking and listened, amused.

"Well, he's in the Army now and would like to get mail. He told me to ask you if you might write to him." She explained, handing me a slip of paper with his address.

This was not an unusual request. Many of the senior girls corresponded with friends or even strangers who went into the service. I exchanged letters with two other G.I.s and Freddie became my most devoted pen pal in no time. He came home for a long weekend and took me out every day. I met his parents, and they were delightful to me. After that short visit, his letters grew more personal, and before long I found I was eager to hear from him.

After Christmas, his sister told me he considered me his girl, but he had not said as much to me. Soon, it was modest love letters coming my way and I was flattered. Unfortunately, though, I didn't return his fervor and continued to date others.

Freddie took me to lovely places during his infrequent furloughs and made a special effort for my senior prom. He showed up with an orchid corsage and was charming to my grandparents. What I didn't anticipate was his gift!

In route to the prom at the Southern Yacht Club, he pulled the car over, parked under a street light at the entrance to City Park, and gave me a small, fancy package topped with an elaborate bow.

"Open this now, Suga. I'm being sent to Germany for the next twelve months and I want you to have this before I leave."

I fumbled with the ribbon and paper, finally got down to a black velvet box, opening it to find a ring with a bluish stone, which I thought was an aquamarine, my birthstone.

"Thank you, Freddie, this is beautiful." I slipped it on my right hand.

"Is that all you're going to say? You have it on the wrong hand." He said.

"Uh, it's very nice, and it fits. How did you know my size? What do you mean 'wrong hand'?" I didn't know what he meant.

"It's an engagement ring. I'm asking you if you'll marry me when I get home." I held it up to the windshield for better light, saw the exquisite blue diamond, turned to his open arms and kissed him.

Père's words about retiring came back to me and I felt I had little choice.

"I will, Freddie, I'll marry you." I answered.

He turned the car around and headed back to the house to tell Mère and Père. They were sitting on the front porch and, obviously, had been in on the surprise. After kisses, hugs, and congratulations, we dashed off to the prom.

Jim was there, as escort to one of my friends. he had the audacity to ask me to dance and I accepted. He admitted that he had called Mary Ann to invite himself, just so he could see me. I told him of my engagement. After our dance, he shook hands with Freddie, congratulated him, properly offered best wishes to me, and walked away.

Excited about the night, heady with my friends' exclamations over our engagement, I was giddy. We got home in the wee hours and Freddie left the next day. We had no time to make formal plans.

A few days before the end of my final year at St. Joseph's in 1954, Uncle Warren asked Mère during dinner what news she had of Bruce and Germaine. I knew they were in the Philippines and were soon to return stateside, to New York.

"I'm sure she spends her days at the Officers' Club," Mère said, "drinking all afternoon. Germaine writes that she fraternizes with her neighbors, strangers, really. How bourgeois!" Mère went into her usual tirade and I kept my focus on my asparagus salad. All eyes were lowered as derisive remarks flew across the table. I caught a grimace from more than one of my aunts. My intuition warned me that I would be the one to upset the equilibrium as my thin veneer of self-control was ebbing like an outgoing tide. I couldn't even look at Mère as she went on, and on, and on to the others. They were obsequious, and accepted all her criticism about Germaine, who had dared to defy her. Pushing my chair back, I stood abruptly, throwing my monogrammed linen napkin into the gravy on my plate.

"Stop it! Stop it!" I turned to Mère at the head of the table. "Why do you hate my mother so much? Can't you ever say anything good about her? About anybody? Who says you can run down everyone? What did they do to you? I won't sit here and listen anymore!"

Everyone was shocked. I couldn't see Père's eyes at the far end of the table as light from the chandelier reflected off his pince-nez. Uncle Warren spoke up, "Now, Lynne, you shouldn't talk to Mère like that!"

"Oh, no? You should hear what she says about you!" I spit back.

Knocking over my chair, I turned and stomped out of the dining room, running through the parlor and up two flights of stairs to my room. Choking on tears of frustration, I threw myself on my bed, hoping no one had followed me. Of course, Aunt Lucy, who took emotional abuse in stride, came in behind me.

"Lynne! You must know Mère loves you, loves all of us, but especially you! We never want to hurt her feelings and you should never talk back! She does so much for you; she took you in when no one else..."

"Stop! Don't play that old song!" I sat up and glared at her.

"Sweet girl, it's the truth, you should love her for it! Nobody did want you! I want you to apologize." She implored.

After she left the room I turned off my bedside light and pondered. *Why am I defending Germaine and Bruce? Are they who I think they are? Do I just really want them to be my parents? And what if they aren't? Could it be Aunt*

Rosie and some man I don't know? Who am I, Blessed Mother?

Obediently, I apologized the next morning. Mère didn't say a word to me for days.

The atmosphere in the Sarrat house had been chilly since I had announced that I was leaving for New York after graduation to join my parents. They had been opposed to my making this trip, but my ticket had been paid for by the Army when Bruce claimed me as a dependent.

What else could I do? I had won a full academic scholarship to Sacred Heart Women's College in Northern Louisiana, but Père didn't believe in women going to college, so he refused to cover my room and board. I wrote to Bruce for assistance; he responded that he would have to provide college funding when Jerry and Tommy were ready. There would be no money for me.

I would have gladly taken a job, but there was no work-study program at the college, and it was so remote, I couldn't work without a car. A car, hah! I didn't even drive. Bitterly, I relinquished the scholarship I had prayed so long and hard for.

Mère offered her usual diatribe about Bruce being a scoundrel. In her opinion he was déclassé, a worthless fortune hunter who couldn't hold a real job.

"You'll be sorry! He'll make you sleep with your brothers in a crowded hovel!" She insisted again.

On a short visit to Virginia I had slept on a sofa in their apartment. After years of hearing all this negativity, I turned a deaf ear. Long ago, I had stopped wondering why the boys lived with Germ and Bruce and I didn't. Were they stepbrothers? Half-brothers? Not brothers at all? No use asking questions, everyone tells a different story, no two of which agree or make sense.

Two weeks later I experienced my first menstrual period and turned eighteen. A woman at last, a little one, perhaps, but all there. I was leaving New Orleans the day after graduation, embracing the opportunity for a chance to live with Bruce, Germaine and the boys.

I was disappointed to learn that they had been in New Orleans for two weeks, staying at Aunt Rosie's, and were planning to leave the day before my graduation. When I confronted her about it, Germaine mumbled, fumbled, and lit one cigarette from the other. Her fingernails were filed to severe points and painted dark red. She looked 'witchy', coughing so much she could barely speak, "Priss, I hope you'll understand, we won't be here when you graduate. Dad only has two weeks before he reports for his next duty station. We want some time to see the sights of New York and look for an apartment, get our feet wet in the big city, see some plays maybe, a Broadway show or two."

Really, I thought, they couldn't stay one more day?

"Goodbye, Muz," I said bitterly, 'I'll see you at Grand Central Station."

I was less than nothing to them.

Upon entering the auditorium, I recalled my first day at the Academy when an elderly nun had warned, to my chagrin, "We knew your mother, little girl, and we're going to watch you very closely."

The highlight of graduation night was that all four grandparents, who had not spoken to each other in eighteen years, were in attendance. They cheered and congratulated each other, waving across the auditorium when the American Legion Award for Leadership and Scholarship was presented to me after I delivered the valedictory address. The principal also presented me with a gold cross and chain as outgoing student council president.

Père stated when we got in his car, "You've paid me back tonight for everything I ever did for you, girlie."

The next day Tomas drove me to the station, and with tears in his eyes, said lovingly, "Take care of yourself, little girl, and pray for old Tomas." We hugged and cried together; the first time he had ever touched me.

My train arrived in New York early the next day. I was surprised that people were wearing somber colors in June, and here I was, decked out in a pink suit of my own design. Self-consciously, I stepped off the coach. My "new" family met me in Grand Central Station. Everyone seemed a bit nervous. Jerry and Tommy each took a bag and we followed Germ and Bruce to a parking lot.

Traffic in New York was worse than anything I had ever seen, and the trip seemed interminable. On the way to their house, Germ rattled on about everything they had been doing, explaining that housing wasn't available at Governor's Island where Dad was stationed, and the apartment they were able to get was at Ft. Hamilton in Brooklyn. So what. Did I know the difference?

My parents were both chain smokers and the car smelled disgusting. I opened a window and feigned interest in the awful view. Tall, gray buildings were jammed together, flashing by like ghostly sentinels. Jerry and Tommy shared the back seat with me, saying nothing, but I felt their angst. I was intruding. I snuck a side glance at them taking in their dark hair, so much like Germ's. Not once did either say a word or look at me. They just stared out the window. *Should I care? What am I doing here? Do these people know anything about me, that I faint and have migraines?*

Then came the bad news, their apartment had only two bedrooms, so I was forced to share a room with the boys. My head spun and my hands got clammy; Mère had been right.

It took two hours to get to our destination. I was expecting a house, not a cluster of high-rises where everyone rode the elevator. They lived on the fifth floor of an eighteen-story building with a parking garage below that smelled like wet cement. I was told this modern abomination was built on the site of an old slum. There were no trees, no gardens or grass, no sign of the lovely neighborhood I left behind.

Inside the apartment the décor was unusual, consisting mostly of souvenirs from the Philippines. Fishnet on the ceiling held Japanese fishing baubles, plastic crabs and fish; not exactly the refinements Germaine or I had grown up with. Overflowing ashtrays covered every table, crowded among brass whatnots, giving the room a curio-shop atmosphere. There was only one bathroom.

My parents occupied the smaller of the two bedrooms, leaving an extra-large room for three of us to share, divided in half by a curtain on a wire. I was given the rear portion with a window overlooking the Narrows, where ships moved in and out of the harbor. It wasn't an ideal situation, but I was learning how to handle things existing outside my cocoon.

The boys were very careful to allow me privacy, which I appreciated. I related to Jerry, who was seventeen, good looking and very kind to me, but Tommy was just a little kid, nine years old. A beautiful hand-carved teak chest, chosen in Manila for my hope chest, was the focal point of my portion of the room.

Jerry offered to take me to a party the first night to meet his friends, and I quickly lost the pink suit and put on jeans. Most of the boys there were my age or older, sons of military families returning to West Point shortly. The girls were younger, still in high school, but more mature than my old friends. I learned we were referred to as "Army brats." Most spoke several languages and had lived all over the world.

One tall, blonde young man, the lifeguard at the base pool, Corby Grundman, was a junior in college and asked for my phone number. The following week Corby took me to hear Dave Brubeck's progressive jazz in Manhattan, and then another date to see Louie Armstrong. Corby was pleasant, but so tall I barely came up to his chest.

Jerry's girlfriend, Pat, also a blonde, became my pal; she introduced me to two of her classmates, Patti V. and Judy, also blondes, and officers' daughters, who were not allowed to date enlisted men. I soon learned they spent their time dreaming up ways to get dates.

What they considered a harmless prank turned out very, very badly. "I have to babysit tomorrow," Pat says, "why don't you three come over and keep me company?" When we arrived, Patti V opened a box of food coloring containing four bottles, red, blue, green and yellow. She passed them out announcing, "This is the plan. We'll each use a different color in our hair and march across the parade field. Surely some cute officers will notice us."

I got the red, which was not so awesome, nor was the yellow; but the green and blue were outrageous. We laughed ourselves to exhaustion. What the girls knew, but I didn't was that no one walked on the hallowed parade ground unless in a parade.

The military police who arrested us were amused when they locked us up in the Provost Marshall's office. Our four embarrassed dads were summoned to bail us out, the others, still minors were grounded for weeks. Bruce was not pleased but imposed no penalty. I had never had so much fun nor so much freedom.

Wearing a faded housecoat, as she did every day, Germ cornered me when we were alone. "Priss, if any of our friends should ask where you've been, we'd like for you to stick to our story, that you were away at boarding school. Our friends don't know you have never lived with us." No one ever asked, so I didn't have to honor their lie.

I was writing letters one rainy day, when Germ asked me to sit down with her again. She indicated a kitchen chair and poured herself a cup of coffee. Stalling, she lit a cigarette while another burned in the ashtray.

"There are things you need to know, Priss. My mother, was very hard on me. Mère felt threatened because my father loved me more than he loved her." She said.

"Are you serious? Why do you think that?" I was appalled, this sounded like an Electra complex.

"This is not all in my mind," Germ continued, "if that's what you think. He showed me in many ways, that if Mère hadn't been there he would have chosen me. I used to wish she would die! I'm ashamed to tell you, but I did."

I was stunned. Can she really believe this nonsense?

"Before you say anything, you need to hear what happened when you were born. My mother was so outraged and angry, she stole you away to punish me. It was her way to get even with Dad because he took me away from her. She never liked me, never liked him, so she took you! They would have allowed me to come back home, if I gave up Bruce. Imagine how hard it was for me? I couldn't do that. I was not willing to live under her thumb. You understand, don't you? I had used your Dad to get away! Do you blame me?" she asked.

"Wait. I'm not sure I understand. People don't 'take' babies from each other. I understood I was abandoned, is that true? What about Jerry and Tommy? She let you keep them. Is it true you lived in a car? Mère said..." I was interrupted.

"Oh, bosh on what Mère said! We had nowhere to go. We tried to get Pauline to take Jerry, but Grandfather Moore told Dad he had to take care of his babies himself and they refused to take us in." she explained.

"You're telling me you tried to give Jerry and Tommy away, too?" I was shocked.

"Priss, try to understand, we did live in a car for a short while. Jerry had just been born. I wasn't working, and Dad couldn't keep a job because Grandfather Moore would call him to take his yacht out. He had to go, or at any rate, he claimed he did. Dad quit several jobs to do his father's bidding for free! Your grandfather conducted business on the yacht when his cronies came to town and Dad loved the role of captain. I had to support us." She said.

"Why are you telling me this now? Isn't it a little late?" I suggested.

"You should know how hard it was. Once we only had money for a box of crackers and a quart of milk, so we gave Jerry the milk and we ate the crackers. We couldn't take care of both of you. At least I knew you were safe." She justified.

This was a lot for me to think about, and I wasn't sure I believed it, but before I could question her further, a neighbor came through the unlocked door holding her own cup of coffee. I was relieved.

"Well!" she said, "I finally meet the mystery daughter. Your mom and I have been friends since we both lived in Ft. Eustis. I'm Midge McCann. My son, Lee, is leaving a week from Thursday to go back to school for his final year. Why don't you come back home with me today to meet him after your mom and I have our coffee?"

Lee was good-looking and very smart. He took me dancing before he returned to West Point and let me know he was looking for a girlfriend, not a bright move. I wasn't available.

Mustering to Germany brought Freddie through New York, and he came to meet my parents. "Now Freddie, I understand you are a paratrooper," Dad said.

"Yes sir, Captain Moore, and in two years I'll be going back to Loyola in New Orleans." He replied.

"Do you and Lynne expect to be married by then?" Dad asked.

"I hope so." Said Freddie.

"What are you going to study in college? And what do you plan to do after you graduate?" Dad continued.

Freddie politely answered, "Probably a variety of subjects, nothing on my mind just yet. When I finish one course of study I'll begin again with another. With the GI Bill, I believe I can get six or eight years of schooling, don't know yet what I'll do."

"So, will Lynne have to support you during that time?" my father asked politely.

"No, sir, absolutely not. No wife of mine will ever have to work." Freddie promptly replied.

We drove Freddie to his ship the next day, and on the way home, Dad summed it up, "Suga, you heard what I heard. This boy is very nice, but unfocused. Your future will be a disaster."

"I know, Dad, I realize that now. We simply didn't think this through. We've had no time, just a year of letters, just twelve days face to face. We didn't get near the subject of marriage or the future. I was swept off my feet when he showed up with a ring. When I get his new address, I'm going to break it off. He forgot his dress shoes, so I'll mail them back to his mother and put the ring in the toe, with apologies."

The base exchange hired me as a sales clerk in the camera department. A young G.I. asked me where he could find the 'pros'.

"Pros?" I asked. "Prophylactics," he said.

"Oh, the tooth brushes are over there," I said, pointing to my right.

"No," and he emphasized "pros, you know." A more mature lady pushed her way between us, whispering something to him about ignorant little girls, as she pointed in a different direction.

A few minutes later he returned and asked if I'd go out with him after work. I politely declined and at the end of my first and only day, resigned.

Against my parents' wishes, I took the subway into the city to look for a job. Bruce lectured me about 'white slavery' which went right over my head. Germ was sure I'd get lost. On the third day, I was riding the subway into Manhattan, circling in red the want-ads that I planned to check out. A funny little man, dressed in fancy vest and spats and holding a Homberg and gray gloves, sat across the aisle. He looked like Edmund Gwenn, the British character actor, who played Kris Kringle in the movie "Miracle on 34th Street. He moved into the seat next to me and my heart lurched like popcorn popping.!

"Young lady," he said, "I see you're looking for a job." He held his black Homberg and gray gloves in his hands.

"Oh, no, not me," I lied, trying to hide my marked-up newspaper.

"Don't be afraid, I just want to help." His smile was disarming, but I was wary. Jumping up, I lied again, "Sorry, I get off here." I had no idea where I was but dashed out at the next stop. He followed me off the train, up the stairs and out to the street, where I slipped into a cigar shop. He followed. I stood where the proprietor was polishing the glass counter. I wanted to make sure he heard every word, if this man spoke to me again.

Coming right up to me, 'Edmund Gwenn' said, "I happen to know Miss Langmier is interviewing at AT&T today, 195 Broadway, 13th floor. Tell her Abraham Simpson sent you." He donned his hat and left the shop. The tobacconist and I looked at each other; he reached for the telephone directory under the counter. "Sure enough" he said, looking up at me, "American Telephone & Telegraph is at 195 Broadway!" he reported.

"And where is Broadway?" I innocently asked.

When I described Mr. Simpson to Miss Langmier at AT&T, she denied knowing him. She was a tall attractive lady, who put me at ease, laughing, "Simpson must have been your guardian angel." She hired me as a 'call girl'; I was to be part of a pool of girls who are 'on call' when anyone on 22 floors was on vacation or out sick, mainly to answer their phones. Call girls also delivered interoffice mail and set up conference rooms. I had trepidations about telling my very nervous father I was going to be a call girl. I did know what that was.

Suga dressed for work in New York

I had a 90-minute subway ride each way, every day, and Dad was sure I would be victimized. He insisted on dropping me off at 6:30 a.m. when he drove in to Manhattan to pilot the ferry back and forth to Governors Island.

I stood on the street until the building opened at 7:30, available to be kidnapped. No one even spoke to me, they just rushed by.

I took the subway home to Ft. Hamilton and after a few weeks, rode it alone both ways despite Dad's fears. Nothing happened.

It was a very nice entry level job, with lots of variety and great girls in my crew. I was a bit of an oddity, coming from the South. They teased me about the way I spoke and looked. These big city girls wore very short stylish hairdos while I had long blonde hair halfway down my back. My clothes had always been homemade, but when I got my first check for $37.50 I bought a few new things and blended in.

Three girls in my office went up to West Point with me for dances on weekends, when invited. We boarded a

Greyhound bus downtown after work on Fridays and took a room for four at the Thayer Hotel right inside the grounds. We found the dances fun with thirty-two hundred cadets who were perfect gentlemen. Upper classmen, especially Lee McCann's friends, were generous and attentive and took my friends and I out when they had holidays at home, in Brooklyn. I encouraged Pat Murphy, Jerry's girlfriend to join us.

Lee and three friends took us out for dinner over Christmas at the Hoffbrau House on 86th Street in New York City. Having spent four summers in Germany, the guys spoke fluent German, so they ordered for us. Excusing himself, Lee went to the men's room and a waiter put a small bowl of red cabbage in front of me. I tasted it, liked it and ate it all before my date came back. The entrées came next, along with special wines, desserts and entertainment by waiters wearing lederhosen and singing boisterous German songs. On the way home, Lee said, "I wonder what ever happened to my red cabbage?" I didn't tell him I had eaten it.

My only reservation about this handsome, super smart guy, was that he was so rigid and formal, and after several dates he still hadn't relaxed and couldn't act like a normal twenty-two-year-old. He was still calling me 'Miss Moore', when he led me to the famous "Kissing Rock" on a mountain path up at the Point.

"Tradition says that any cadet who brings a girl here has to kiss her. If he doesn't, or she refuses, he's a loser." He stated.

"Really? Are you a loser, Lee?" I teased.

"It's up to you. May I kiss you, Miss Moore?" he asked politely.

"Sure." I replied.

Lee attempted to kiss me but forgot to take off his cap. It had a large hard black visor, which hit me on the forehead and knocked me back a step. He laughed, apologetically, but didn't try again.

After I had been in New York only eight months, Elaine, my friend since kindergarten, called with a big surprise. "Can you believe I'm getting married?? His name is Bobby and he's in the Coast Guard. Will you come home to be my maid of honor?"

"I will, on one condition." I answered, "You must promise not to tell Jim I'm coming."

"And why not? He asks about you every time I see him." She said.

I was adamant, "Just don't, please, he broke my heart."

Although the Sarrats knew I was coming home for Elaine's wedding, I hadn't let them know my $35 redeye flight landed at 2 a.m. Rather than disturb them at that hour, I took a taxi from Moisant Airport, pulling up in front of the house at 3 a.m.

A man was sitting on the broad front steps, his elbows on his knees and his head on his crossed arms. He was wearing a suit, so I assumed it was one of one of my uncles who had forgotten his key. I paid the driver and as I got closer to the steps, the man stood up, and I was surprised to see it was Jim!

"What are you doing here at this hour?" I kept the mood low key, but I was shaken.

He took my suitcase and purse, set them down, and taking my hands, drew me to sit with him on the cold marble steps. The porch light was off, but the moon was bright. "Suga, your father called me. He didn't know what time you might arrive. I've been here since nine o'clock. I want to ask you not to go back to New York. I've been out of my mind dating girls just to win a stupid bet with George when all I want is you."

"Whoa, Jim. You've caught me off guard," my head felt light and my heart pounded like a jack hammer.

"Why are you surprised? I put this in both my letters and your responses were so positive."

"I didn't write you a word, James Mouton! Listen, I'll be here a week for Elaine's wedding, we can talk about it later."

"I don't think you know how much I care for you, Suga, there will never be anyone else." His familiar arms went around me.

"Jim, I'm going to admit something I never thought I would. Over this last year I dated a lot and compared each young man to you, but sadly, nobody quite measured up."

"Does that mean you've thought about me?" His lips hovered over mine for a moment.

"I tried not to, but, yes. Oh, yes!" He kissed me long and deeply, no longer the kiss of a boy. He held me for a long time. Though I relished his embrace, it was well after 3:30 and I was exhausted.

Later I thought, *why did he say I had answered his letters?* Letters had come from Jim, that's true, but I tossed them, unopened. Months later, I learned that Dad was pirating the trash and typing responses in my name. He had met Jim only twice but had been very impressed.

A call came the next day from Thomas Finney, one of Jim's closest friends. "Lynne! I heard you were back home! Will you go out with me tonight? I have to broadcast a basketball game at Loyola at seven. Jim and his date will pick you up and we'll go slummin' together after the game."

Jim came for me in his father's car and claimed his date was sick. We had time to kill until Thomas finished broadcasting, so he took me to one of our old haunts, a smoky little club called 'C'est Soir,' where our crowd had danced for years. When we danced it was like old times, and Jim got serious. "Suga, will you take this until I can afford a diamond?" He was holding his fraternity pin, offering it to me again.

"Wait, was this a set up?" I asked.

"Guilty as charged. Finney will get over it," he replied.

We had a drink, then another. We never got to that game at Loyola, staying until the club closed. I never went back to

New York and Thomas Finney never spoke to either of us again. We shared the guilt.

I transferred to Southern Bell in New Orleans as a clerk in the directory department. Jim had a job at a shoe store on Saturdays and full time all summer; both of us banking the larger share of our checks.

We coordinated lunch hours when possible, walking a short block into the French Quarter to have a Po'boy sandwich at Felix's Oyster House. During the depression, a few restaurants put a slice of ham or cheese on French Bread for the poor for 10 cents, hence the name, "Po'boy."

A strange young man who worked with Jim, often came with us, although we never sat together. He chose to take his oyster Po'boy outside, where he backed up to an exterior wall and slid down to a squat, sitting on his haunches. Always alone, he rarely had much to say during the walk. Most of what he did say was mumbled, making little sense. We called him Harvey, but his full name was Lee Harvey Oswald. After the Kennedy assassination, we heard his name repeatedly in the media, and Jack Ruby killed him before our eyes on TV. We couldn't believe that introverted and pathetic boy had committed such an outrageous, shocking crime. Jim mentioned this to a professor, a Jesuit priest, and his advice was to 'keep our own council'.

"Don't talk about it," he said, "the world is in such an upheaval over Kennedy's death. There might be more crazies out there, and to admit you knew Oswald might put you in jeopardy." We kept quiet for several decades about having known him.

Mère secretly offered Jim a diamond ring that had been passed down in the Michel family. The one carat diamond was in an old-fashioned setting, so she encouraged him to have it re-set for me. Here was a loving and benevolent side to Mère that I had seldom seen.

Our friends celebrated our reconciliation with toasts and good wishes, but the reaction from my family was even more enthusiastic. He had endeared himself with his demeanor and work ethic and my uncles and Père were wholeheartedly behind us. The women thought he was God's gift.

In November, Jim told me to get 'gussied up,' as he had made reservations at the Blue Room in the Roosevelt Hotel. Rusty Draper was singing, 'Lover Come Back to Me' when, at the stroke of midnight, Jim pulled out a blue velvet box. He proposed to me and put the fabulous ring on my finger.

Having completed his sophomore year at Loyola, we planned to marry the following spring. We worked toward his graduation together, capitalizing on my scholastic gifts and his determination. I composed so many of his papers I felt I was earning the degree, too, but was happy to do it. With a year to plan our wedding, we also planned our future, including lots of children. The first thing, though, was for Jim to graduate and find a job.

Chapter 7

We hit a roadblock when we went to apply for the $2.50 marriage license. Neither of us could produce a birth certificate. Jim had been born in the country, near Lafayette, where births weren't recorded in 1934, and I had never seen my birth certificate.

Germ had rented an apartment in a renovated grand old house for herself and the boys nearby until they could join Dad in Alaska, and she wanted to participate in the wedding plans. Within walking distance now, she came to have coffee each morning with Père, while Mère spent the early part of each day giving orders to the help, and having her hair and nails done. Germ walked in through the rear entrance, and up the service stairs, careful not to cross her mother's path. She was habitually disheveled, wearing scuffed shoes, tight slacks and a wrinkled, untucked blouse. In one hand she had her coffee cup, in the other, a cigarette.

She came up to my room when I was getting ready to go to work, putting on my lipstick. "Good morning, Priss."

"Good morning, Muz." I told her of the futile visit to the license bureau. "So, what should we do?"

"Priss, there has to be a way, but I've never seen a birth certificate for you." She said.

A chill went down my back and I confronted her. "I have to know. Is it true that you left the hospital after I was born without paying the bill or taking me?"

"We're not going to go into that right now." She was adamant.

"Someday you'll have to tell me the truth, and this is the day!" I was resolute.

"Don't ask me what I did when I was 16!" she protested.

I was just as firm. "But Muz, I must have a birth certificate! I have to leave now, or I'll be late for work." I headed for the door, pulling the strap of my purse over one shoulder.

"Let me try to help," she suggested. "I'll get in touch with Rosie."

"What does she have to do with this?" I asked.

Without responding, Germ called and left a message with Auntie Rosie's answering service as I bounded down the stairs. When I got home that evening, there was a message from Rosie.

"Germ, I got your call. I asked Father about Lynne's birth certificate. He said all documents are locked in his safe. His lawyer has to work with it first, then he'll give it to me."

I was nonplussed after hearing an attorney was 'working' with my birth certificate! What does that mean? And why did Grandfather Moore have it in the first place?

Other things took precedence and the issue of birth certificates was tabled. Eventually, Auntie Rosie did whatever it took, and we got the license. It said Lynne Moore was born February 29th, 1936;(we had been celebrating my birthday on March 1st.) Germaine Sarrat and Bruce Moore were named as parents. They hadn't been married.

I began my wedding dress alone, using an empty room. Amélia tacked white sheets to the walls and floor to keep it pristine; my dress form, whom I named, 'Godiva' stood in the center. Draping and experimenting, I tried many options, the fabric in my hands guiding me.

The dropped bodice fit my narrow waist snugly. It was topped off with a low scooped neckline and small sleeves, shaped into scallops, high on my arms. The hem, including the train, was enormous, and was made by hand. Mère had purchased the bolt of exquisite fabric I had chosen, but her hands were her real gift. Every evening for a month, Aunt Lucy gingerly carried the gown downstairs and spread it across our laps as we sat at either end of a sofa. We sewed in opposite directions, using tiny invisible French stiches. When we met, the thirty-six-foot long hem was complete. Never once placed on a hanger, the dress came to fruition in three months. I removed it from Godiva every free moment to work on it, no matter how briefly. Showers and parties took up weekends, plus I had a job and Jim was busily wrapping up his third year at Loyola, so time was precious. Finally, I sewed two thousand seed pearls on the dress and fingertip veil, until I was satisfied.

Wedding Day
May 30, 1956

This was the first wedding dress I had ever made, but certainly not the last. Years later, when I had to support my children alone, that gown served as inspiration for many others, bringing rich rewards.

I chose to have Germaine on the altar as matron of honor. Only one special seat in the church was allocated to the mother of the bride, and Mère had earned that privilege.

Père would give me away, and Bruce was so offended that he refused to even request a furlough. Was I his to give away? I had lived with them for only eight months.

Much frustration and discussion ensued about invitations, so I had them printed, "Captain & Mrs. J. Bruce Moore **and** Mr. & Mrs. Pierre Sarrat request the pleasure, etc., etc."

"How many invitations may I have for my list?" Germ challenged Mère one morning.

"Germaine, you know very well the Moutons will be given half." She replied.

"That won't be necessary, Jim's mother told me she only needs fifty for their family and business associates." Germaine informed her.

"Well then, you and I can divide the remaining 350 since Lynne ordered 400 from the printer." Mère relented.

"I don't think so. Lynne and Jim have friends, and he belongs to a fraternity." Germ said, obviously baiting her.

"Emily Post suggests we expect three attendees for each invitation. Holy Rosary church will hold 600 people, and we have handled that many here in the house for receptions. So how many do you absolutely need?" Mère wanted the last word, causing World War III between them.

Each morning when I came down to breakfast, one or both was crying; the other making ugly remarks about the names on each list. Mère contended that Germaine's friends were in foreign places and could not attend. Germ's argument was that Mère's list contained society snobs and ancient half-dead relatives. This volley went on for days. When I had heard enough, I interrupted.

"You will both stop this now! Before I'll listen to another word of this rubbish I'll call it off and we'll elope!" I headed for the door with the two of them in pursuit.

"You'll see," I called over my shoulder, "I'm going out on my lunch hour to buy a dress you'll never see! Jim and I are going to get married tonight." I did buy a dress, a terrific navy-blue sheath, with a white chiffon jabot, but capitulated when they pleaded with me, both of them contrite and ravished with tears.

Mère cried "Ever since you were a little girl, I have dreamed of seeing you go down the aisle in a dress you designed and made yourself!"

"Please, Priss, we'll settle our differences, please don't run off," Germ said.

The navy-blue dress was saved for my 'going away' outfit.

An entire salon on the first floor of Père's house was cleared for the hundreds of wedding gifts. A special staff was hired to catalog all the crystal, silver, china, household appliances, mirrors and objects of art, plus scores of linens to be displayed. Security personnel remained on site during the wedding and reception.

May 30th, 1956, at 5 p.m., a stretch limousine delivered four stunning bridesmaids in pastel gowns to the manse, while my portrait was being taken. The little flower girls, Betty Ann, 8, and Jeannie, 4, giggled when I told them about how I had ridden in the limo jump seats when I had been the flower girl in each of their mothers' weddings.

Mère left in the first black Lincoln and the bridesmaids followed. The final limousine, reserved for me, Père, and the flower girls, waited at the curb. The driver tried to assist me into the back seat but the hoop skirt under my dress was larger than the open door. In an effort to help, Père pushed with his foot, breaking one rung of the hoop, which I took in stride. We were finally settled in the silent, luxurious car. I was jubilant, and nothing would bring me down on this day.

Our driver apologized for the multi-block traffic jam along Esplanade Avenue approaching the church. Many guests had remained outside, wanting to see the bridal party arrive, but the back-up caused Père great anxiety. "Driver," he said, "let us out here, we'll walk the rest of the way."

"Ma Père, Non! We are not walking. We'll get there when we get there! They can't start without us." Could I see myself walking down the sidewalk with two little pink angels skipping alongside? FOR FOUR BLOCKS??

Having done this so many times with his daughters and nieces, it was no wonder Père wanted to get it over with. I took his hand in both of mine and he relaxed. "Père, this moment is a gift, really, a time for me to thank you for the wonderful life you've given me."

"Mon Chere, you needn't thank me. Mère and I have been so happy over the honors you've earned, and the way you've conducted yourself. I think of you as my daughter, and I have never regretted the night I walked out of that hospital with you in my arms. You have been our joy." He reached over the volume of flowers on my lap and kissed my hand. "God bless you, my girl, be happy for this old man."

I blotted the tears from my eyes with the tissue Aunt Lucy had pushed into my glove along with an ammonia ampule. She had seen me faint at my first communion, confirmation, twice at Elaine's wedding, and many times in between.

Eventually we got out in front of Our Lady of the Holy Rosary Church which has been compared to the lavish cathedrals of Europe. Those standing on the steps and the large circular approach to the street, pulled back and made way for our entry. Camera flashes burst on all sides as I stood in the vestibule, conscious of the enormous crowd facing us. I watched the pink, blue, yellow and green gowns go slowly down the aisle followed by two precious little pink ones. After a calming, deep breath, my foot touched the long white cloth leading to the altar. How many times had I walked that aisle, I wondered.

At that moment, in her exquisite soprano voice, my dear friend, Sandra Scafide, began the Ave Maria from the choir loft, and I was launched down the aisle on Père's arm. I made a conscious effort to turn on an imaginary tape in my head, a record that would remain forever as Père escorted me with dignity down the endless aisle. Every face I saw was forever ensconced in my memory.

I noticed sadly that only Auntie Rosie and her little girl, Denise, attended from the Moore family. There had been some hard feelings when I didn't include any other cousins after Auntie Hazel critically made some demands about my plans and color scheme. She had pulled her daughter, Hetsy, and her son, Butch, from our bridal party. Their absence sent a message, but my wonderful Auntie Rosie didn't let me down.

I spied Jim and his groomsmen, including our three brothers and a fraternity brother, in pristine white tuxedo jackets. Papa lifted my veil and kissed me, placing my hand in Jim's, then winked at us. I remained upright the entire time. Father Palughi conducted a poignant and lovely service. Fully aware of the vows I was taking with the man I loved at my side, I was sure we were doing the right thing. Only time would tell.

The Sarrat House

We came out of the church in a blitz of rice, tumbling into the waiting limousine. We arrived at the house n a blur of flowers, kisses, and good wishes. We took our places in front of a massive mantle, eager to receive our friends. We were handed champagne, toasted, sipped. We were congratulated and took hundreds of compliments. Guests were still lined up beyond the doors when I was abruptly removed from the reception line by Nannan Hilda. “You have a phone call, Suga.”

“You’re kidding me,” I tried to say over the violin music and hundreds of voices.

“It’s Bruce calling from Alaska.” She managed to get me and my huge dress to the phone in the dining room where the regal eight tier cake seemed to glow. I was not thrilled as I took the receiver and she attempted to direct people away from me, so I could speak. There was static and interruptions by an operator. A voice finally said, “Go ahead, Alaska.” I was able to make out a man’s faint voice thousands of miles away.

“Mrs. Mouton?” Sounded like he was under a pile of debris.

“Yes, is that you, Dad?” I asked.

“I wanted to be the first to call you by your new name.” he said.

“Thank you, Dad, but I can’t talk right now, it’s terribly loud in here and I’m supposed to be...” I protested.

“What?” he asked.

“There are hundreds of people here, all waiting for me to return to the reception line.” I tried to explain.

“Let them wait, you’re being congratulated by a “Bird Colonel”, I just got a promotion because I’ve been working on the DEW Line here in Alaska.” He crowed proudly.

“That’s great, but Dad the reception has begun, and I need to...” I was again interrupted.

“How does it feel to be a married lady?” he asked.

“I haven’t had a chance...” I tried to reply.

“Mother told me you made a beautiful dress.” He said.

“Yes, I guess I did.” I answered plaintively.

“Tell me about it. You make me so proud with the things you design and sew.” He went on.

"Thanks, Dad, but this is not the time..." I said firmly.

Every word and phrase had to be repeated over the static and I was frantic. I couldn't get him off the line. I knew he was sorely disappointed I hadn't let him give me away, but that would have been a farce. After a long string of questions about our plans for our honeymoon and Jim's future employment, all punctuated with much static and repetition, my tears of frustration began to flow. Finally, Germ made her way to me through the crowd and said, "Is that Dad?"

"Yes!" I gratefully handed her the phone, asking her to apologize for me. Aunt Lucy was nearby and wiped my tears, smearing my makeup, but I didn't care. Fighting my way through the milling guests who all tried to stop me to talk, my fingertip veil became dislodged and I caught the headpiece in my hand. My hair was a fright. I got to Jim who also had questions I couldn't answer. Half an hour later I was seeing the last of the line as they offered their best wishes. I had missed most of it. Eventually, we moved into the dining room to cut the cake.

I was relieved when Mère made her way to me and removed the orchid corsage in the center of my bouquet and said we should head upstairs to get ready to leave. By then, it was nearly nine o'clock. Pausing on the red-carpeted stairs, over the banister I looked at the sea of faces. I tossed my bouquet and Jim threw my garter to the eager young men. A valet led Jim to the room where his clothes were laid out.

In Mère's bedroom, which had the only window air-conditioner in the house, the bridesmaids helped me out of my gown and into the navy-blue dress. I made a bun of my long damp hair and put on a flat little white hat. In later years the children laughed when they looked at our photo album and said. "Mom wore a Chinet plate on her head to leave her reception!"

Ready to go, Jim rejoined me on the second-floor landing where I spent so much time eavesdropping as a child. Amélia was standing back in the shadows. She blotted her eyes with a crumpled handkerchief and reached out to touch me on the shoulder in a loving gesture. I grasped her fingers in mine and choked back a tear before we reentered the reception, knowing there are as many forms of love as there are moments in time.

More rice accosted us as we ran to an outrageously decorated car driven by Jerry. Many friends followed, leaning on horns all the way, tailing us downtown to the Roosevelt Hotel where we were let out. The followers struggled to park for a shivaree, but we dashed through the lobby and out the back of the hotel. There, thanks to Jim's brother, Rodney, our best man, the actual getaway car was parked, packed with our bags, champagne on ice, and a box of cake and sandwiches. We headed for the Gulf Coast. By midnight Jim was signing in as Mr. and Mrs. at the White House Hotel on the beach in Biloxi, Mississippi.

Two nervous virgins found themselves alone in a hotel room on the third floor. The bellhop hoisted our luggage onto the bed, accepted a tip from Jim and left, abandoning us. Tension filled the room like smoke, eating up all the air. Avoiding Jim's eyes, I opened my suitcase, unsure of what to do next. Did we make a mistake, remaining ignorant, chaste and celibate? I was completely unprepared for what was supposed to be a magical night. Should I ask him to wait until tomorrow? What should we do to get this wedding night going? Jim solved the issue temporarily, by saying, "I'm going to take a shower," and left me standing in the middle of the room.

I changed into my lacy white nightgown and waited, sitting on the edge of the bed, nonplussed when I heard the water turn off. What comes next? I had brushed my hair one hundred strokes. Should I do it again counting by twos? Jim came out of the bathroom, wearing blue pajamas, grinning sheepishly. He climbed into bed without a word. He wrapped his arms around me; I put aside the hairbrush and snuggled close to him. My first shock was experiencing the thinness of only two layers of clothing between our bodies!

We kissed and fumbled and eventually copulated. Neither of us took off our nightclothes. It was uncomfortable for me, but that only lasted a few minutes. I was not remotely aroused when he shuddered, rolled off and kissed me goodnight. Still, not a word. Is this supposed to be a silent activity? Dr. Charbonnet had examined me so many times, that there was no blood, as I was told to expect.

When Jim turned off the light and turned away from me, I could see a full moon through the window, thinking, if this is 'it' why does everyone make such a big deal over sex? I would spend the next thirteen years initiating love making, knowing that I craved something, but never understanding what it was.

Later in our marriage, Jim became a traveling salesman. When he came home off the road, he would be annoyed at my amorous greetings and accused me of being 'all over him'. His joke was, "Wait, let me put down my suitcase." His lack of sex drive reinforced my sense of rejection; particularly when I learned within two years that he was seeing other women.

It was tragic that his frigid mother had taught him that sex was shameful, dirty, a sin, and he must go to confession anytime he gave in to his instincts. *Why do I feel so alone?* Mère's ominous words were carved into my soul like a gravestone, "**Nobody wanted you**."

Chapter 8

Germ wrote that she was "pregnant at age forty." Suddenly, I had a new clue to my past. If she was forty and I was twenty, she could not have been sixteen when I was born. Bruce claimed to be the same age as Germ. How old was Rosie? There was no excuse for twenty-year-olds to abandon a child. They weren't desperate teenagers, she wanted only him.

Unfortunately, Germ had a difficult time and gave birth to a stillborn baby girl, christened Pamela Ann. When I learned I was pregnant, too, she returned the maternity dresses I had made for her.

My healthy son, James Edward III, arrived on March 29th, 1957. He looked like a tiny version of Grandfather Moore, fat, blonde, and red faced. I counted his fingers and toes and let the nurse take him away, then I slept off the long laborious night.

The next day Mère came to the hospital and showed me how to nurse him. I will always love her for that. It's a place that has no name, a place where no one could ever come, a place where we're alone, yet together.

The challenges of cooking, cleaning and laundering convinced me that no child of mine would grow up ignorant like me. Over-indulging a child is not a gift! Living in a tiny apartment at Père's house gave me access to the help who made every effort to assist me. Mère's washwoman washed much of our clothes with theirs, and Mary often saved us leftovers. Nevertheless, I attempted to become self-reliant.

My worst fiasco left me scarred and wiser. I ran through the back yard to Mary's kitchen door. "Mary" I cried, "how do you make French fries? I cut the potatoes up the way I knew they should look, threw them into the pot, but..."

"First you get the grease hot," she offered.

"Grease? Oh, Mary! I had a pot filled with boiling water!" I turned and ran back to my kitchen, threw out the water and melted some Crisco. I then threw the wet potatoes into the hot grease. Jim came home and found me in tears, my arms spattered with burns.

Eddie was two months old when he attended his father's graduation from Loyola University. Soon after, Armour and Company hired Jim for a sales position in Texas and we eagerly prepared to move. Jim and I didn't know what we didn't know. The pay was $90 per week, more money than we had earned when we were both working. In 1957 that was decent entry-level pay for a salesman walking away from college with little experience behind his BA.

Having rented a one-bedroom, two-story townhouse through a friend in Houston, sight unseen, Jim and I drove out of the Sarrat's compound in our second hand, gray, 1953 Dodge. Mère, Aunt Lucy, Tomas and Amélia stood in the drive bawling their eyes out.

Eddie traveled well in his car bed in the back seat. We packed some diapers, a few clothes, a box of miscellaneous supplies, and an old Army cot, which Père had contributed. Off we went on our own with an 8-week old baby, whom I had been afraid to bathe, frightened that when he got slippery with soap I would lose him in the water. In lieu of a bath, I rubbed him all over with cotton balls soaked in baby oil until he was ten weeks old.

In the cardboard box from home, the bottle sterilizer, coffee pot and three Pyrex covered dishes were a godsend. I heated soup and Chef Boyardee meals in the coffee pot and we ate out of the Pyrex. Eddie nursed, ate from baby food jars, took his juice in bottles, and thrived.

By the third night Jim and I experienced red spots and itching, which we tolerated, but the baby screamed constantly until Jim called an exterminator, who discovered the apartment was infested with fleas.

Jim went out on the road exploring his territory, leaving me alone with the baby. Time to take a step forward. Our transportation consisted of my two feet and a stroller. I jammed diapers around Eddie, so he could sit up, then ventured outside. Exploration revealed a little park with swings and a seesaw, St. Patrick's Catholic Church, a mom and pop grocery store and a laundromat, all within walking distance.

Finally, a phone was installed, and I managed to get registered in our parish. By the third week, the furniture arrived, along with cold weather. Delighted to see the sewing machine I had bought myself, I gave it a position of prominence in the living room. Bored and wanting to see somebody over two feet high when Jim was traveling, I pushed Eddie's stroller across the street to the little market, put a few grocery items into the basket behind my bundled-up baby boy, and went into the laundromat. Crossing the street and making the sign of the cross, I posted a 3x5 card stating a bold exaggeration, "DRESSMAKER," plus our phone number, and posted it on the bulletin board.

I headed home, saying the Hail Mary. I asked the Blessed Virgin to help me start a little business of my own. I had every confidence that Mary was watching from her perch on my shoulder.

Using the Yellow Pages, I phoned seamstresses to see what they charged per job and set my prices at one dollar more. I had learned from Mère that many women didn't believe things were good enough for them unless they paid a high price. By the end of the week I had received three calls and had three clients! When the ladies who called inquired, "Can you make this?" or "Can you alter that?" I answered yes, because I believed I could figure it out. I altered, patched, hemmed and stitched, making some "pin" money. Each job taught me something, because I examined details of each garment and learned how designer clothes were made. I never disappointed my customers. In fact, each brought new business.

In November, I experienced hard cramps, and passed a bloody blob which I scooped up into a jar. I called a new friend I had met at church, who picked me up. She took care of Eddie, while Doctor West determined I had suffered a "spontaneous abortion". He sent me to the hospital, because the baby I lost was one of two, apparently from separate conceptions! So, I was still pregnant.

On December 1st, 1958, Armour. dissolved their soap division, and with Jim's next check came a pink slip. The entire crew of soap salesmen were out of a job. It would be costly to move back to New Orleans.

A.J. Thompson, an old friend from school, also living in Houston, offered us an option, "Jim," he said, "how would you like to come to work for me downtown?"

"Doing what?" Jim asked.

"I need an assistant manager. I can't deal with the hours when Christmas rolls around. Come work for me and I'll teach you the ropes." He offered.

The position at W.T. Grant, a five and dime store, offered less money, but I was hoping he would be home every night. However, the worst challenge was still ahead.

On New Year's Eve we moved again, this time to a larger, less expensive two-bedroom house, all on one floor. Eddie at ten months old was walking and curious. It was easier to handle him on one level, plus we rejoiced over the fenced-in yard. I canceled the diaper service and bought a washing machine. Anticipating the birth of our second child in June, Jim strung four clotheslines in the yard, for twice as many diapers. Let's go, Blessed Mother.

Early spring of 1958 brought a call from Alaska. "Priss, it's Muz. We're coming back to the states. Dad was reassigned, and we want to come to Houston to meet our new grandson. Do you have room for us? We won't stay long, Rosie is expecting us in New Orleans for our month-long R&R."

"I can offer you a king size sofa bed, will that be all right? We have an army cot for Tommy." Jerry was then a freshman at LSU. "Muzzer, do you think you could stay until the new baby arrives? I need someone to look after Eddie while I'm in the hospital. Jim can't take off from Grants."

"We'd be happy to babysit our grandson. We'll love it." She replied. Days and then weeks passed, but no baby. No doubt she wanted to eat those words. They let us know how unpleasant it was on our sofa and complained about the social affairs they were missing in New Orleans.

We had put eight names in a hat and let Eddie choose two for the unborn baby. So his little brother was named "Peter Randolph," and he spoke of him as "Bebé." He came on June 4, 1958 and was christened immediately so that they could leave.

Jim's parents, whom Eddie called 'Paw-Paw' and 'Mae-Mae', came to Houston for Thanksgiving to see the new baby. One night after dinner, Paw-Paw said, "Suga, why don't you let us take you and the little boys back to New Orleans to visit your grandparents for the month of December? Jim thinks he'll be working seven days a week until midnight."

Jim chimed in, "Thanks, Dad, Suga needs a break and I won't be any help at all with my schedule. Grant's will be open every night until Christmas. To tell you the truth, as good as the kids are, they are squealy little boys and I'll be glad to get them out of my hair."

My Sarrat grandparents were retired in Bay St. Louis, now, and were eager to see their first two great-grandsons. Their former summer home had been a playground for me as a child. Père had built quarters for guests and the help who accompanied them. Often, I was allowed to bring Elaine and we walked the beach, played ping-pong at the Bay-Waveland Yacht Club, and compared our tans.

This visit was different, I was not a teenager anymore, but the mother of two boisterous little kids. I kept the boys busy outside when possible, not wanting to disrupt the folks' idyllic life.

By the time the boys and I flew home on December 23rd, I learned I was carrying another baby. Jim had to send someone to pick us up at the airport because the store was so busy. Happy to be home, I knew Jim would be as delighted as I was that we now had the possibility of adding a baby girl to our little family. I fed and bathed Eddie and Bebé and put them to bed.

When Jim hadn't come home by 1 a.m., concerned, I called the store. Willie, the night guard, answered. "Willie, this is Mrs. Mouton. Is my husband still there?"

"No Ma'am, everybody's gone." He said.

"Thank you, Willie. You have a Merry Christmas." I was frightened. If he had been in an accident, I prayed he was still alive. Life without him wouldn't be...well it wouldn't be life.

Next call was to his boss, A.J. "No, Suga," A.J said. He and I closed the store together about 11:00. Maybe he had car trouble. If he's not home in an hour, call me back."

Just before 2 a.m., I heard a car in the drive. Frozen in the chair, I knew if the doorbell rang, it would be the police. I heard the key turn. The door opened quietly, Jim was standing there, face drawn, his suit jacket hanging on his frame. I kissed him and took his coat, shocked that his shirt collar was standing away from his neck.

“Didn’t you eat while we were away? You’re a skeleton.” I stated, concerned.

“I ate. I need a bourbon.” Was his reply.

“Sit down at the table.” I put a slice of Mère’s cake and a cup of coffee in front of him, hoping to sit and talk a bit, ready to blurt my surprise, but he cut me off.

“Suga, let me talk before I lose my nerve.” He was haggard, pale and his eyes were brimming with tears. Wearily, he slumped in the chair across from me at the yellow chrome table. I stirred my coffee and waited, but he didn’t speak.

Finally, I asked, “Is something wrong?” He had a hard time bringing his eyes up to meet mine. “Please, darlin’,” I whispered, “whatever it is, we can handle it.”

“No, we can’t.” He pushed the cake away.

“So, tell me what’s up. I know you didn’t lose your job because I talked to A.J. tonight.” I said.

“You called A.J.?!” His face flushed with anger.

“Well, yes, I was worried.” I answered, confounded by his temper.

“You shouldn’t have brought him into this,” he shouted.

“Into what? What, Jim?” I asked.

“There is no other way to tell you, I got somebody pregnant and I think the honorable thing for me to do is to marry her!” He blurted.

“Marry? Marry? Are you kidding?” I raised my blouse and showed him my baby bump. “Know what this is?” When he offered no response, I remained silent a long moment to mask my reaction, letting the shock fall away before my mind moved into gear. But before I could speak, I laughed, breaking the silence. His expression morphed into a contorted strain, and as blood rushed to his face I almost felt sympathy for the poor fool. He let out a rasping sound and cried in anguish. His rush of tears came next.

It was not the first time I had heard that nobody wanted me, but this was not about me. My mind took over and I knew I had to take charge. There would be no time for anger. There was more at stake now. “What are you telling me, Jim? You have a girlfriend?”

“I never meant for it to go this far; there’s a girl at the store that I’ve been driving home. One night her boyfriend’s truck was in her driveway, and she said he’s a big brute and she was afraid of him, so I kept on driving and brought her here… a few times. I couldn’t resist, she’s beautiful She helped me buy a Christmas tree and decorate it.” He offered lamely.

“She slept in our bed? Who is she?” I asked seriously.

“What? That’s not important, Suga.” He attempted.

“You screwed her in our bed?” I asked.

“Her name is Betty McKenna. She works in cosmetics. You’ve never met her.” He explained.

“Tell me you didn’t fuck her in our bed!” I repeated.

“Don’t use language like that. You don’t talk that way.” He answered righteously.

“You don’t like my language, but you have the gall…” I couldn’t get over his nerve.

“Well, yeah. I didn’t bring her tonight because I didn’t think you’d understand. I let her off at her house. I stayed a while because she’s scared of him. She’s young, and she’s afraid.” He said.

“So, you had to rescue her? Is that your job, Jim?” I asked, suddenly calmer.

“Please. Suga, I didn’t think at all, and you were away…” he offered as an excuse. Jim cried silently, letting the tears pour from his half-closed eyes and down his face.

Standing up, I took one of his hands in mine and led him out of the yellow kitchen and down the hall. When we came to the boys’ room I clicked on the light. They didn’t wake up, sleeping like puppies in their little jammies with rubber feet. I gently picked up Eddie and handed the limp toddler to Jim. Bebé, I placed in his other arm. He looked dumbfounded glancing down at his sleeping sons in his arms.

“Now tell me that again?” I whispered softly, “Who you got pregnant and what’s the honorable thing to do?”

He miserably placed the boys back in their baby beds, still sleeping. All he said to me was, "Damn! You sure know how to hurt a guy." I closed my eyes for an instant, keeping my mouth shut. We tiptoed silently back to the kitchen, the expression on his face was pure pain.

"Go to bed," I told Jim, "I'll take care of this." I regretted those words the moment they were out of my mouth. I was letting him off easy, giving him a license to cheat. Would he do it again? Not only had he betrayed us, but now it was in my lap. He turned silently and headed down the hall to our bedroom with a sigh. Jim slept like a baby when he hit the pillow. I remained sleepless.

After he left for work the next morning, I called our sitter and headed for St. Patrick's where the pastor let me pour out my grief and overwhelming renewed abandonment. "What can I do, Father? How can I fix this? Please?" Now I was crying.

He spoke gently, "Don't worry. I'll go to see him, ask him to take a walk and talk to me. Here's what you won't like; you're going to have to forgive him, but you'll never forget it. My advice to you is to never, ever bring it up again. Can you promise me that?"

"Yes, Father, I'll do anything to save my marriage." I replied.

"Go in peace and pray for him." He said.

I put in a call to Jim's dad in New Orleans as soon as I got home. "Paw-paw, this is Suga, we have a problem."

"What's that, Darlin'?" he asked.

"It's Jim. He's taken up with a woman... a girl, really, and she claims she's pregnant." I replied.

"Oh, no! Are you okay?" he questioned.

"No, not even close. I just found out that I'm pregnant, too." I was miserable.

"Don't worry, Suga, Mae-Mae and I will be there by tomorrow at the latest." He promised.

After his father and the priest spoke with him, Jim agreed to give up the girl. Jim's mother confessed to me secretly, "His father did the same thing to me."

"And how did you handle it?" I asked.

"I haven't let him touch me in nine years!" she smirked triumphantly.

The night after his parents, returned to New Orleans, the wall phone in the kitchen rang. Jim raced for it, but I was closer. A female voice asked for Jim and instinctively I handed it to him.

"It's for you." I said.

I went through the swinging door into the living room, but spun and pushed back through, snatching the receiver from Jim. "Who is this?" I demanded

"Betty McKenna," said the girl.

"Listen, young lady, you talk to him on your time at the store, this is my time! You will <u>not</u> call here and I'm hanging up on you!" Slamming the phone back in the cradle, I turned to Jim and hissed, "Don't let that happen again!"

His tears flowed again; he looked beaten once more. I had not believed the girl was pregnant and I was right.

A customer was due for a fitting the day after Christmas, so I had to put on my dressmaker face. I wished Mère could see how her training was appreciated. I wrote to her of my gratitude for what she had taught me; but she never responded.

Weeks and months passed, and between diapers and feedings I thought a lot, and talked to myself in a mirror. I had lost my sparkle. Here I was, bereft of the radiance that defined my life until then. I couldn't claim to be a good wife with dishes in the sink and dust bunnies under the furniture. Blundering through half-assed cleaning, putting all of my energy into baby care, I was in my third pregnancy, loving every minute of it, but that was all I knew, and it wasn't enough.

I was just hanging dozens of Birds Eye diapers on the line, barely learning to cook and manage a house. I saw myself, no longer a girl, but not quite a woman. I had to take control of my future. I had to get rid of self-defeating dialogue when it seeped into my consciousness. Jim's rejection colored my brain function, but now was not the time to feel sorry for myself!

Chapter 9

Bruce had shipped all the baby furniture they'd never use, so we then had two of everything. Eddie and Bebé sat side by side in their high chairs in the sunny kitchen, spaghetti sauce all over their bibs, noses and chins. Learning to feed themselves was a mess, but a necessary, happy mess.

Doubling up in pain, a single cry escaped me. "What's the matter, Mommy?" Eddie's little brow wrinkled. "Mommy?" Echoed Bebé. Eddie stood in his chair and I helped him climb down to the floor, wiping up as I went. I couldn't lift him anymore, he was too heavy, and I was six months along. No sooner had Eddie's feet hit the floor than I was jolted by another hard, familiar pain.

No! I can't be in labor! Six months is not enough! I won't give up my baby girl!

I sat on the floor beside the high chairs, resting my elbow on a lower rung, gasping, "Run next door, ask Mrs. Rogers to come quickly."

Jim was parking in the drive when Eddie came back pulling our neighbor by the hand. I was vomiting in my own lap. Poor little Bebé was distressed, still buckled in his chair.

Many hours later when we returned from the hospital, Mrs. Rogers had the boys bathed and sleeping. Jim paid her while I groped my way down the hall and into bed. He came in and looked down at me. "What are we gonna do? I can't take off work for three months for you to remain off your feet."

"I don't know! I've never threatened to miscarry before, why is this happening now? We have to keep this little girl we've prayed for!" I replied.

Jim's first thought was to call Germaine in Alaska for help. He was sure she would come to Houston to care for me and the boys. She absolutely refused to leave Bruce. Jim ran up an outrageous phone bill for two weeks begging her while he used up his vacation as caregiver. He wouldn't give up. Finally, Bruce and Germaine offered to send money for someone to come in full time, so I could take it easy until the baby came.

A huge woman's body filled the bedroom door. She was so black her patent leather skin shone. Large white teeth, like Chiclets, poked out from her big smile. She had to weigh four hundred pounds, size 52, the dressmaker in me surmised.

She greeted me, "Good morning, little Mama. I's Helen. I's here to make sure you gets dat baby girl!" She cooked wonderful meals from scratch and handled the little boys beautifully.

After fumbling through Eddie's first year, Bebé was a breeze; weaned, potty-trained, and out of his baby bed within a year. Thank you, Blessed Mother. His personality was pleasant. He was a smart little guy, devoted to me, as much as Eddie was devoted to mischief.

I questioned Helen at length, and in exchange told her stories of our lives in New Orleans.

"If'n you was raised like a turnip, who tole you 'bout babies and house makin??"

I confessed I was only beginning to learn.

She continued, "Miss Suga, dat's one fine lookin' man you got, but tell me, how comes he sens his white shirts t'da cleaners?

"Oh, Helen, he sends them out because I make a mess of them." I answered.

"We gonna fix dat." She promised.

Helen lowered the ironing board and pulled it up to where I sat on the side of the bed. Her demonstrations proved to be fun and I learned quickly. Daily, Helen took the boys for a walk to show them the gifts of nature. "Lil boys," Helen told them, "After I's gone, you remember Old Helen when you sez dem prayers e'vry night."

"Don't leave us, Helen," they chorused!

She stayed for six weeks after Jane Gabrielle was born on July 20, 1959.

The Blessed Mother chose the pinkest, happiest little 8 and 1/2-pound beauty for us. Mrs. Rogers came to the hospital with a special gift, a tiny pink 'girlie' dress, size 6 months. Jane was so small, she wore it for her one-year photo, looking like a doll. Miss Jane had curly blonde hair and brown eyes like Eddie. Bebé's eyes were blue like mine. Jane immediately took over the boys' hearts.

We had agreed that Jim's friend, George Saltzman would be the baby's godfather, and we'd name the baby after him When she turned out to be a little girl, he had to wait until next time for a namesake.

Wanting to go back on the road, Jim took a job with Lever Brothers, who moved us to Mobile, Alabama.

Jane's first birthday arrived, and Aunt Lucy rode a Greyhound bus to spend the weekend with us. Dropping the boys at a day nursery, Lucy and I took the out to lunch. Jane was so excited to be in a restaurant and rose to the occasion, waving and smiling at everyone who passed. Afterwards, we ambled through Bellingrath Gardens with Jane asleep on Lucy's shoulder, until I was exhausted. Heading home, I took a wrong turn, got hopelessly lost, and drove for another hour, getting back to the day nursery as the sun was going down

All the other children had been picked up and Eddie and Bebé were alone in the dusty yard, clinging to the Cyclone fence, their dirty faces streaked with tears. They were whimpering pitifully, their voices raspy. Having suffered with abandonment all my life, I took this to heart and I berated myself mercilessly. I could never erase that image of my babies' fear that they had been forgotten.

After only four months, Jim proved himself invaluable to Lever Brothers and was offered a larger territory in Arkansas, beginning immediately. I was only days away from delivering our fourth baby, so I had to go it alone after he left. Neighbors helped me and Leslie Anne home from the hospital the day after her birth on October 28, 1960. Looking more like me than the others, she was fair, with wispy blonde hair, blue eyes, and a tiny frame.

The big kids and I worked all night, less than a week after Leslie's birth, as it was my practice to leave a house immaculate. We spent the final night in the empty house on blankets on the floor after the movers left.

Jim only had a brief time off and arrived at dawn after having driven all night to get us. He collapsed after we secured the kids in the car. Binding up my breasts so they wouldn't leak, I drove for six hours, stopping only once to nurse and go to the bathroom, until Jim felt rested enough to take over.

We beat the furniture to the house he had rented in North Little Rock, Arkansas, so we spent seven nights in a motel with Leslie in the little car bed that had brought Eddie to Houston.

Leslie was reluctant to eat and suffered from diarrhea. She began to lose weight and I knew something was seriously wrong. Rather than keep the three older kids closed up in a motel all day, I found lovely Ms. Broyles next door to our empty new house. She agreed to take care of them in her home. I kept the nursing baby with me, but she never cried and didn't want my breast milk.

"Can I give you a piece of advice?' Mayola Broyles asked when she saw Leslie. "Get her in to see my Doctor Chudy, he'll get her going. How much did she weigh when she was born?"

"Eight lbs. two ounces." I responded. Mrs. Broyles put Leslie on her baby scale. At three weeks, she was down to 5 pounds, 3 ounces and ghostly white.

"Take her today, don't fool around." She called her doctor and I went right to him.

"Dr. Chudy, what's wrong with my baby?"

"I'm sorry to tell you, dear, this baby has amoebic dysentery. She's not strong enough to handle it. I want you to go straight to the hospital; I'll call ahead to tell them you're coming."

Our baby sitter in this new town turned out to be a godsend. She kept the three big kids, while I moved into St. Vincent's hospital with the baby and Jim continued to explore his new territory. He was reluctant to tell his manager what we were dealing with.

In the ER, IVs were immediately inserted into both Leslie's legs after her tiny fragile body was taped to an upside-down Y-shaped board, to keep her immobile. For ten days, she lay silent and feeble. I was frightened when Dr. Chudy appeared to despair.

"Mrs. Mouton I think you need to face facts. You're going to lose this baby. I doubt she'll last the night. Do you have anyone who could come here to be with you, your mother, perhaps?" Germ and Bruce were once more in transition, staying at Rosie's. I called from the hospital. "This is critical, Muzzer, they think the baby's going to die. I need you to come here, please?"

"Oh, no, Priss, I'm sure she'll pull through. Dad leaves for overseas in a week and I can't leave him now. Say a prayer." Was her solution.

Leslie survived the night. The next day I called again, "Please, I'm begging you, Muzzer, I can't face this alone. Jim's on the road."

"Now listen, Priss, she didn't die when they said she would. Have faith, she'll get better." She said.

One more day, and I was given no hope. The other mothers with children on the ward were sympathetic and a priest spent some time with me in Leslie's room, He was a short, compact man with a perpetual five o'clock shadow. "Do you want me to speak to your mother?" he asked.

"Oh, Father, would you? She's not taking me seriously." I dialed the number and gave him the phone.

"Her name is Germaine Moore," I whispered to him.

"Mrs. Moore, this is Father Jerome. I'm here at St. Vincent's with your daughter who needs you very badly." He said.

"Are you sure the baby's going to die, Father?" Germaine questioned.

"I'm not a doctor, but the thinking here is that the little baby can't last another day." He replied.

"We just can't arrange it now, Father. I'm sorry." She said.

"I'm going to pray to the Blessed Mother to take care of your daughter and her baby, but I wish you'd reconsider." He implored.

"Please understand, Father, I can't. Please help my daughter to understand, also." She hung up.

I stayed at Leslie's bedside and slept on a cot in her room, only washing up in the sink and eating cafeteria food. I spoke to the boys and Jane at Broyles' house every day. They were well fed and wore clothing outgrown by her kids.

"Muzzer," I tried again, "Can you please rethink this? I'm alone and the boys and Jane are with a stranger." This was a tug of war I felt I was losing.

On the fifteenth day, Father Jerome and Dr. Chudy convinced Germaine and Bruce to come Leslie turned a corner and began to improve. Germaine was noticeably irritated,

"There! I told you. She didn't die after all." They left the day I brought Leslie home.

I was thankfully greeted with a clean house at our destination. The movers had placed all the furniture in the living room and I arranged the house with help from Mr. Broyles and one of his sons. My boys helped unpack all the boxes. Jim came once, just for overnight, and we settled into our new digs and adjusted to the cool fall weather. It would take at least a year to build up a profitable sewing clientele, especially since we lived in a town where fashion was forgotten.

I soon realized that with four kids and doctor bills I'd have to go out to work. Mrs. Broyles took care of the children and I landed a position with Arthur Murry Dance Studio, paying $15 per hour, a fortune in 1960. They gave me the equivalent of a $40,000 crash course while making me an instructor. As soon as I completed my training I was promoted to Guest Director, receiving bonuses for every walk-in or student's guest I signed to a contract, in addition to teaching.

Eddie fell out of the top bunk and broke his collarbone in March. We switched the boys' beds, so he wouldn't have to climb the bunk bed ladder. At three, Bebé was a little warrior who relished hopping up into the top bunk.

Early Easter Sunday morning, Eddie tiptoed into our bedroom and tried to wake Jim. He touched his father's face and Jim opened his eyes.

"My bed is on fire, Daddy," he whispered into Jim's nose.

"Go back to bed, Son, your bed's not on fire. The Easter Bunny is still sleeping, give him a few hours." Jim said.

Eddie went back to his room. A few minutes later he was back, this time to my side, "Mommy, wake up, my bed is on fire."

"Go back to sleep, Eddie, it's too early and your bed's not on fire, you had a dream." I offered.

"It is, Mommy." He insisted.

"No, darlin', not possible." I said firmly.

"But, Mommy, there's fire and Bebé's in the top." He persisted.

I staggered to my feet as he took me by the hand and led me to his bedroom door. Opening it, I stepped back in horror. Roaring flames licked up to the ceiling from the bottom bunk. Jim, following me, reached out and slammed the door.

"Too late, close it off!" he shouted.

"Bebé's in there!" I screamed, opening the door again and stepping into the inferno.

"Bebé! Bebé! Are you up there?" Smoke was trapped near the ceiling. The vaporizer I had left on for Eddie was melted on the floor near the lower bunk. I got as close as I dared, with sheets and blankets aflame.

"Bebé! Answer Mommy! Are you in there?" From deep under his old, thick wool-nap army blanket, I heard a muffled little voice cry out, "Mommy! Mommy!"

"Jump, baby, jump out, Mommy will catch you." My brave three-year-old leapt out into the air, slammed into my chest, clinging to my neck like a monkey.

"Mommy, I was scared – it was hot, like fire!" I backed out of the room still holding him. Jim was in the hall with Eddie. I barked at him, "NOW close the door!"

I led both boys to the kitchen where the phone was on the counter top and dialed "O". An operator answered immediately, "Fire at 942 Wilson Drive, North Little Rock," I announced, then hung up, slapping at the singed hem of my nightgown.

I went into the room where both the little girls slept, stacked folded diapers in the bottom of a laundry basket, then put five-month old Leslie on top and called to Jim, who was in the hall holding both boys' hands.

"Here!" I handed him the basket with the baby, "Take her and the boys out of the house. I took Jane, who was barely awake and calmly walked her outside of the burning house.

We settled on the front steps trying to calm the children, waiting in our pj's as the North Little Rock volunteers jumped off the truck before it even stopped rolling. Jim pointed to the window where smoke was escaping, and the men dashed in, some still in pajama shirts. In no time, they had the fire out using chemical tanks.

Since the damage was contained to one room, we were able to stay there, despite the acrid smell. The landlord was reluctant to repair the damage until I withheld the rent check for two months. Jim went on the road and didn't argue. The rent was paid when repairs were made.

Chapter 10

I was under contract to Arthur Murray, Inc. and had to repay $40,000 if I quit in the first two years. Long hours, four children under five, and an infrequent husband, caused migraines again, and I became seriously stressed. Jim only seemed to come home at my most fertile time each month, so I got pregnant again. We were Catholic and didn't use birth control. Thankfully, pregnancy was the only excusable clause in the contract that allowed me to give up teaching.

Jim was blissfully unaware of what stress was doing to me, or what I was doing to myself. Migraines and sleepless nights were the least of it. I took combinations of drugs to rest when I could, and it was never enough. I trembled and shook, and when I found myself calling the children by the wrong names, I wondered if I was going mad. Weeks turned into months, and I was losing myself in a drug-induced haze.

Mayola Broyles showed up and helped bathe and feed the children occasionally. I don't recall eating anything but ice cream or toast during this time, and never when she or Jim were in the house.

The Moutons
Christmas 1960
North Little Rock, Arkansas

My weight had dropped to 107 while I was teaching dancing, but when Mayola made me stand on a scale six months later, it had slipped to 105. I had no idea what to do, nor did I care. I dared not get behind the wheel but took taxis when I had to go out for anything when Jim wasn't home.

Attempting to beat the system by going to three different doctors, I asked each for a prescription for Valium. Foolishly, and not aware of the consequences of what I was doing, I then filled them at the same drug store. The pharmacist, Mr. Carter, eventually called our parish priest, who called our neighbor, a lawyer named Charlie Brown. I opened my front door at 9:30 p.m. one night to find all three men standing on the stoop under the yellow bug light.

"Lynne," Charlie said, "We want to see the children."

Wearing faded wrinkled clothes, my hair askew, I showed them three sleeping children. "Where's the fourth?" Father Wilson asked. Totally confused, I admitted, "I don't know. The last thing I remember was sending them out to the back yard this afternoon because the baby needed to sleep. Bebé and Jane came back in to eat supper before dark, but I can't remember seeing Eddie again."

"Where is Mr. Mouton?" one of the men asked.

"On the road... he travels." I was growing frantic, afraid of what else they would ask.

Father Wilson directed the other two men to canvass the neighborhood, while he stayed to pacify me. Mayola told them I had been in the yard earlier, screaming at 3-year old Eddie to be quiet. She then saw me hit him with a whiffle bat and throw him over the fence. Mayola brought him in and calmed him down. She fed him supper and let him fall asleep on her sofa. She was very empathetic when she told them, "I was only trying to help. Lynne has more than she can handle."

"We'll take care of things, Mrs. Broyles," Carter, the pharmacist, assured her.

He thanked her, picked up the sleeping boy and carried him home. I was relieved to see my big boy. He climbed into his bunk after a stop in the bathroom, seemingly none the worse for wear.

"I'm going to find your husband and get him home." Charlie Brown said, "Try to relax, Lynne, and give Mr. Carter any pills you have."

The following night Jim drove in, furious at being called home for a helpless wife. His supervisor, however, was more sympathetic, offering him a transfer back to New Orleans where our families could help us out. He accepted. Jim suffered agonies of insecurity and fear of losing his job. He started to stutter and drink to excess. I had no reason to think he was cheating again. Just prayed he wasn't.

Grandmother Moore and Auntie Rosie offered solace to me, took us in, and were always ready to take care of the children when I had a doctor's appointment, or just needed a rest. Rosie assumed the role of mother to me and grandmother to my little ones. I can recall many occasions when she contributed greatly to the fabric of my life as I was growing up.

I couldn't have been more than twelve or thirteen when Rose enrolled me in a charm course. I was taught poise, how to gracefully walk, sit, stand, and get into and out of a car, all general ladylike demeanor.

When Mardi Gras season rolled around, she had me stand in for her when Iris and Venus, the two prominent women's Mardi Gras crews, had parades and balls. Rose had participated for decades, but she was getting on in years. Climbing ladders onto a float, standing for hours while tossing beads and trinkets was out of the question for her, so I took her place. She still came to the balls, however.

Finding a nice affordable house with four bedrooms and a finished attic playroom in Jefferson, we moved in December, after two months in Rosie and Grandmother Pauline's loving care.

I climbed over packing boxes when I was ready to deliver the fifth baby and climbed over the same boxes a week later to bring little Mignon home. Jim, of course, had been on the road all week.

Mignon Pauline, born December 21, 1961, our third little girl, was named for her two great grandmothers. Decidedly, she was too tiny for that big name, so we nicknamed her, 'Missy'. She was petite and perfect. Louise Donovan described Missy to perfection when she wrote of Cajun beauties in her book Winds l'Acadie; "The owl-like brown eyes fringed in long black lashes dominated the delicate pixie face."

Rosie, bless her, cared for the others and brought them home only after I was on my feet. Betty, my flower girl, was now old enough to be this baby's godmother. Missy would be her flower girl when Betty grew up and got married. If fate hadn't intervened, Missy's wedding would have Betty's little girl sprinkling rose petals down the aisle. Who could have imagined we'd never see that day?

My friend since kindergarten, Elaine, came to see our new house and two-month old baby. We spent time catching up. Eddie, 4, and Bebè, 3, asked permission to go across the street to play cowboys in a vacant wooded lot, all fitted out in their cowboy gear. Jim and his dad were up on tall ladders painting the front of the house. They could see and hear the kids and promised to help them cross the street when they were ready to come home. Jane and Leslie played with their dolls on the stoop in the warm February sunshine.

After an hour Bebé had had enough and decided to go home alone, although Eddie tried to stop him, knowing the rule about crossing without adults. They argued as far as the curb, but Bebé dashed out from behind a parked car and he was hit and tossed violently into the air by an oncoming car!

From upstairs where I was nursing Missy, Elaine and I heard a loud thump, followed by a child screaming. I looked at my friend and said in a calm voice, “Bebé’s hurt. That’s him crying, I know it!” I handed the baby to her, buttoning my blouse as I ran down the steps and out the door. I passed Jim and Paw-Paw before they could climb all the way down their ladders. Adrenalin driven, I moved toward the woman driver who got out of her car, came around to the front and picked up Bebé. She was covered with Bebé’s blood and brain matter when I grabbed him away from her, and promptly punched her in the face. Who knows what drove me to that!

Ignoring the little girls, I snatched up a doll blanket from the front step and wrapped it around the gaping wound in Bebé’s head. He was conscious and screaming, his cowboy shirt covered with blood. The two men hit the ground running for the car. Paw-Paw jumped behind the wheel of our Ford station wagon; I pushed Bebé into Jim’s lap in the passenger seat. Quickly, they backed out of the drive and headed toward Ochsner Hospital, two miles away.

I turned to look at the woman who had hit my son. She was elderly and obviously distressed. A large white bandage covered one eye. She abruptly pulled it off and dropped it at her feet. We later learned she had no driver’s license and had recently had cataract surgery. She should never have been driving!

Elaine was downstairs by this time, carrying the baby. "I called the police," she said as she handed Missy to me. I led Jane and Leslie, into the house, then quickly dialed Rosie to ask if she would come get the children so I could go to the hospital. She picked up the girls and called Aunt Cyril to come for Missy. I had no time to pump breast milk. Cyril would have to make-do with formula. I also called the parish asking for a priest to meet me at the ER. Instead, Father Ropolo came to the house and took me to the hospital.

Eddie was traumatized, having watched this nightmare unfold. Elaine found him standing at the curb in front of the vacant lot, holding Bebé's little cowboy boot, and waiting for someone to help him cross the street. Stunned and silent, he had witnessed his little brother being hit and thrown by the car, heard him screaming, saw the blood, and was now standing alone. Elaine went to him, dried his tears and took him home with her. Her boy was also three and a half years old.

Dr. Kirgis spent hours trying to save Bebé while Jim and I sat, keeping watch and praying. "Please tell me he's going to live." I begged Jim in the waiting room.

"I didn't look closely, but brain matter was all mixed with blood. I've never seen anything so horrible. He could be a vegetable, Suga, we have to be prepared for the worst." He said.

"I hope he isn't suffering. Oh, God, please don't let him die!" I muttered.

Jim said, "I made him sing little songs to calm him down in the car; we were there in less than fifteen minutes and miraculously, the surgical team met us at the ER door."

"Rosie!" I recalled. "I called Aunt Rosie and she said she was going to call Dr. Kirgis, her neighbor. He is a neurosurgeon on staff here!"

Six hours later, Homer Kirgis finally appeared in the waiting room. He informed us that our little boy had survived so far, and that the next few hours would tell what the future held. It had taken six hours to pick skull fragments out of Bebé's brain, suture it closed, and cover the wound with a flap of skin. There was no longer a protective skull under there.

"Go home and get some sleep if you can." Dr. Kirgis said, "He'll be in recovery all night."

"You go home first," Jim urged me. "Get something to eat and try to rest. I'll be here."

At home, I found his mother roaming around the house muttering that she wasn't going to get any dinner. She had slipped off track during menopause, and was still a stuttering, helpless wreck ten years later. I took covered dishes containing vegetables out of the fridge and put them on the table. "Here's the roast from the oven, Mae-Mae," I told her, as I lifted the heavy pan from the stove to the table. "These veggies are washed and ready, but you'll have to heat and serve them yourselves." She looked away.

I asked her to slice the roast and make a sandwich for me while I was in the shower, putting bread, a jar of mayonnaise and a knife on the table for her. She was incensed and threw the jar of mayonnaise at me. It hit the wall behind me with a big bang, shattering into a million pieces, spraying a mess on the wall and the floor. Saying nothing, I turned and walked out, without a shower or food, and drove back to the hospital.

Father Ropolo and Jim's dad were in the hospital parking lot preparing to go back to the house. As I passed them, I said, "I'm sorry, Paw-Paw," I was shaking, "but you're going to have to get your wife out of my house and don't bring her back! She's a loose cannon and I will have to give all of my attention to Bebé." He understood and nodded.

With the children farmed out, I kept vigil at the hospital, but Bebé was in an ICU and I was only allowed ten minutes every hour to hold his limp little hand and talk to him. He was in an induced coma and didn't respond. The bandage on his head was as big as Mahatma Gandhi's turban, and his eyes were black and swollen shut. Aunt Lucy came to relieve me every day while I went home to shower and eat. My milk had painfully abscessed, but eventually the pain in my breast began to subside. Aunt Cyril had Missy on formula and said she was doing well; sleeping all night.

I implored the Blessed Mother, holding my rosary in my hand, saying prayers between pleas. “Mary, you see what’s happening here. Please give me back my Bebé? Please don’t let him be a senseless cabbage. I have five children and will probably have five more. Please let me see him wake up and hear him say ‘Mommy’ again.”

On the tenth day a nurse came out of ICU and asked, “What’s a hoppy? Does he have a pet rabbit”?

“No, it’s his favorite little plastic Hopalong Cassidy on a horse. Why?” I asked.

“Can you go get it? He sat up and is asking for Hoppy. I’m calling Dr. Kirgis.” I wept as I dashed home.

The next day, interns from the major hospitals in New Orleans were summoned to observe this child with the side of his head destroyed. With only engorged purple slits for eyes, he had arranged pillows and blankets into a mountainous terrain and was sitting up, galloping Hoppy back and forth in his bed.

When the bandages came off, he wore a surgical cap for months. He underwent several more surgeries. The challenge was to keep him reasonably quiet once he went home. It wasn’t practical to simply put a metal plate in the head of a three-year-old, as he would outgrow it and require multiple replacements. By researching both our families, the surgical team was able to estimate roughly how big Bebé might grow, and they designed an experimental, hard silicone plate that overlapped the opening. It was connected by wire rings on all sides to the remaining skull, and as he matured it slipped into place, exactly filling the space. Thank you, Blessed Mother.

He was left with an unsightly scar from his eyebrow, reaching up into his hairline, curving over and down behind his ear, following the contour of the headlight that hit him. Years later, while he was in medical school, a fellow student, studying plastic surgery, obliterated the nasty scar.

Bebe and Eddie

Bebé was quickly approaching school age. Jim and I agreed that his nickname could potentially bring him grief from his classmates and certainly would look foolish on his college diploma. We decided to start using his given name, "Peter," and began the process of weaning Eddie and Jane from using the pet name that Eddie had bestowed on him.

Eddie was a clever child and missed nothing! One morning, keenly aware of the attention bestowed on his brother, he announced, "When I get hit by a car I'm going to get lots of presents and get my head shaved, too." I went right to Woolworth's, bought little cars and books, and then took him to a barber who shaved his head.

"Now you don't have to get hit by a car, see?"

In the years that followed, Peter had several visits with Dr. Kirgis. He declared, "Doctor K, I want to grow up to be just like you, a 'brain doctor' who puts boys back together when they run in front of cars."

He advised, "Peter, you'll have to take lots of mathematics, science and languages in school and learn to play the piano for dexterity in your hands to be a surgeon."

"I will, Dr. Kirgis, and when I graduate, I'll come to work with you in your hospital," he declared. Sadly, Homer Kirgis didn't live to see him go to college.

We couldn't afford a piano or lessons, but the next house we bought had a piano in it, and the owners asked if I'd mind if they left it behind. I taught all the children to play and Peter helped put himself through college playing in a lounge in Tampa. I think we had more than one guardian angel.

A month had passed after we brought him home. Aunt Rosie and Uncle Al brought Leslie home one Sunday afternoon. Jane was already back with us. With tears in her eyes, Rosie explained. "Lynne and Jim, we see history repeating itself. We'd like to keep Leslie forever, but it would be just like you, Lynne, remaining with the Sarrats. I still see you when you were that age, and Leslie's the image of you. We've grown to love her like our own and if we don't give her back now we never will be able to give her up."

Jim and the children and I welcomed Leslie home. Jane, especially, was delighted to have her little sister back. Perhaps I had been neglectful not getting her home sooner. I wonder if Germaine once registered the same regret.

I went to visit Grandfather Moore when he was in the hospital, dying. He looked pitiful, half his normal weight.

"How many children do you have now, baby?" he asked.

"Five, Grandfather." I replied

"Have one more for me, baby, I had six." He suggested.

Grandfather's wish inspired us to discuss our little family. As Catholics, we had not used birth control, but stress and the medication I had been given after Peter's accident had inhibited my getting pregnant. What if God had another one or two babies for us and we failed to accept them? Would we be denying our child? We agreed that I would get off the pills. Jim promised that he wouldn't cheat anymore. I wanted to believe him.

Elaine visited me again the following year, and we went to see Amélia. She had retired and was bedridden, living with a niece who was at work at the time of our visit. A neighbor let us in, then slipped out to her home, next door. We spent the day with Amélia, feeding her some special things we brought and giving her a sponge bath. Elaine had gone through nurse's training and knew exactly what to do. I sang the little French lullabies my devoted mammy had so often sung to me, and she was pleased. She fell asleep, and as we were leaving her neighbor looked in and smiled her approval.

"Oops," I said as I pulled away from the house. "I forgot something. I always let her know when I'm expecting."

Elaine gasped, "You're not PG now, are you?"

"I most certainly am. This one is due on Peter's birthday in June."

Eddie had been frustrated in kindergarten, just as I had been, waiting for the other children to learn what he already knew. Being a less aggressive little girl, I had waited patiently, but by second grade Eddie grew restless. He had books beyond his age level to keep him busy, even the Reader's Digest, but he was still bored and looked for more adventures.

Once, the fire department took him off a ledge encompassing the second story of the school building, and he never revealed how he got out there. His teacher told me when she would pin a note to his shirt that read *"Parent: please call me for a conference."* He would unpin it and pin it on another kid. I never saw a note, while other parents were going to unnecessary meetings.

I invited six of Peter's 's little classmates to his birthday party on June 4th. The kids had a great time. That night, I went into labor, probably brought on by hosting those boisterous little boys in my backyard, while I ran up and down six steps, in and out of the kitchen.

We had agreed the baby would be named after our friend, George. He would at last, have his namesake and he would be godfather. I was still heavily sedated when I was told by a hospital volunteer that we had an 8-pound baby girl.

"And what will the baby's name be?" she asked.

As Jim had wearily sat by my bed through twenty hours of labor chanting, "Come on, Susie Q, come on, Susie Q," I groggily replied, "Susie Q".

"No, really? the woman asked, "What about Suzanne?" Not in the mood to argue, I snapped, "Fine, can I sleep now? Oh, and her middle name is George. Make that Saint George."

A few days later, when Jim brought me and the baby home, Eddie, Randy, Leslie, and Missy were sprawled on a huge Early American braided rug, engrossed in the Mickey Mouse club on television. Four-year-old Janie was rocking in her little chair with gusto. Aunt Lucy peeked around the door from the kitchen. We stepped quietly into the room, and only Jane looked up at what I was holding in my arms.

"Is that for me?" she questioned as I gingerly put the baby onto her lap saying, "This is Suzanne." Jane's arms encircled the infant, "No, Mommy this is Pookey Baby, I'll take care of her."

Suzanne's first words were, "Pookey Mama". She remained, of course, "Pookey Baby" for life. Jim and I called her, "Suzi," a nickname stolen from Elaine's last child.

I had taken each of my babies to Amelià for her to hold. That simple act meant so much to each of us. When she died, over a hundred years of age, Nannan called me to say that the whole family was going to pay their respects. The funeral home was in a solidly black community. They had a small, pristine chapel, with glowing statuary and candles along the communion rail.

No one expected the reaction when we walked in, Amélia's white family. The people in the chapel became silent, sensing who we were, and stepped aside, making a wide aisle for us to pass to the front. One at a time the Sarrats and Leaumonts, my aunts, uncles and cousins, knelt at the prie-Dieu to say their goodbyes. When it was my turn I lost my composure, throwing myself across Amélia's body in the coffin, sobbing. Uncle Donald and Père pulled me away and escorted me out a side door. I was inconsolable, feeling I had lost my mother.

Chapter 11

On a warm spring day, Jane found three pennies in the grass while she, Leslie and Missy were playing in the back yard. I was tending to Suzi's bath time and the boys were in school. She had taught Sean, our Great Dane, to lift the big latch on the six-foot gate using his nose, because she couldn't reach it, and he let them out. Holding hands, they walked two blocks to the corner grocery store. It was where I shopped, and Jane always got a penny from me for the gum machine. She was four, Leslie, three, and Missy, eighteen months, so in her little mind, she was the person in charge. No one noticed these three little girls alone in the store on Jefferson Highway and no one noticed that when they came out, they turned in the wrong direction to go home, heading instead, toward Baton Rouge.

Minutes later, I came outside, only to find the gate was open and Sean asleep beside it. I checked over the fence in the neighbor's yard, but no girls. Frantically, I went next door and asked Mrs. Betancourt to sit with Suzi while I scoured the block. I ran up and down the neighborhood shouting for them, but they were not to be found.

I had bathed Suzi at one o'clock, and it was now two-fifteen. At two-thirty, I called the police, and two officers came immediately, took descriptions, and told me to stay home. They soon reported finding one white high-top toddler shoe in the parking lot at the grocery store and brought it to me to identify. It was Missy's.

Beside myself, I phoned Jim and he came home immediately, then left to drive up and down neighboring streets, desperately searching. I was hysterical. Jim was furious with Sean.

At six o'clock a police car pulled up and officers helped the girls out. Missy's diaper was soaked, dragging the ground, and all three were filthy. They had been picked up at Moisant Field (now Louis Armstrong New Orleans International Airport), three miles away. Their route, Jefferson Highway was the busiest main artery between downtown New Orleans and the airport.

Jane couldn't understand why everyone was so concerned. Unflappable, she said, "I don't know why you're so upset, Mommy, I held their hands." She told us that when she discovered Missy's shoe was lost, she made her walk with one foot on the paved highway and the other in the grass. She walked between them, Leslie on her right and Missy on her left. Jim and I wore them out with hugs and tears.

In November of 1963, President Kennedy came to New Orleans to give a speech, and the motorcade traveled that same Jefferson Highway. Eddie and Randy were in school. I put Suzi and Missy, one behind the other in the stroller, took Jane and Leslie by their hands and walked two blocks to wait with other neighbors who wanted to see JFK pass by in an open car.

I attempted to impress upon the girls who he was. The motorcade passed slowly, giving the girls a good look at the president, and they clapped enthusiastically with the crowd. He appeared tan and robust, smiling and waving to my little girls.

After his speech, he flew back to Washington, and the following day Jackie accompanied him to Dallas where he was assassinated. I broke down and cried for Jackie when I heard it on the news.

Things between Jim and me continued to decline. I didn't mind that he spent so much time on the road and at the golf course, I was happily busy caring for the children and sewing for customers. Our problems grew from not being able to agree on anything. This was compounded by the fact that he still felt he had to lie to me about his whereabouts and plans.

All his life, his father had ruled his family with an iron hand, and although my Jim attempted to emulate him, he wasn't around enough to maintain control, nor was he his father. Our intimate moments were even more disenchanting. I confess my complaints and criticism demeaned Jim until he was ineffective.

When Eddie's second-grade teacher suggested we should have him evaluated for constant distraction and mischief, I set up an appointment with a child psychiatrist. Jim considered this a waste of time and money. On the second visit, she offered him a piece of chalk, a large slate, and asked him to draw himself.

"And what did he draw?" Jim asked.

"Just a huge head, eyes, nose and mouth, taking up the entire slate. He sees himself as just his brain, and assumes that's his only value to us, according to her," I replied.

"So, what are do we supposed to do about this?" Jim was not impressed.

"She told me, first, you simply acknowledge small accomplishments. He's old enough to set the table or read to his baby sisters. He can help put away groceries or sweep the walk. Positive reinforcement. But the major thing she wants us to consider is a school for gifted children. She said the state of Louisiana will educate him through college at no cost to us, if we allow him to board at a special school."

Jim was totally negative. "Are you nuts? I'm not letting him go away to a school for geniuses. I'm just average and he'll have to learn to be average, too. No! He's only seven years old. He stays home and goes to Catholic school like you and I did."

"But Jim, she warned me that he'll be in trouble by fourth grade if we don't do this. She claimed he could even be failing by that time. Why don't we go and speak with Father Ropolo?" I suggested.

"No, and I don't want you to go, but I know you will anyway, so satisfy yourself. Eddie is no genius." he declared.

Father Ropolo did not support the idea. In fact. he said Eddie should stay in parochial school and that if he didn't, he wouldn't allow him to make his first communion in the spring.

Like a fool, I gave in, and did nothing, a terrible injustice to our child. The psychiatrist was right, and it cost Eddie so many years of floundering, in and out of trouble, ending in reform school. I can't forgive myself for not overriding Jim and our pastor. Neither one accepted the fact that I had been gifted. Certainly not a genius, but gifted, nonetheless. I made one "B" on a report card in 13 years of school.

I realized that Eddie had pressure heaped on him too soon. By the time he started school he already had four younger siblings, so every step of the way he was warned to behave, lest he be a bad example; not that he listened. Add to that all our relocations. He attended seven schools by the time he was in 8th grade, but still made remarkable grades.

Eventually, Jim was tapped for management at Lever Brothers, with a big raise in pay and no travel. Thank you, Blessed Mother, and while you're at it, please help me move six kids and a Great Dane to Georgia.

As usual, Jim went on ahead. I was president of the PTA, and my final meeting turned into a farewell party. Board members jubilantly escorted me to the airport after a few bottles of champagne and poured me onto a plane. Jim took me out for dinner after he met my plane in Atlanta, amused that I was tipsy. The children had been left with Rosie until we got settled.

Our first rental in Southwest Atlanta had once been a Boys' Club, only one block from the Joel Chandler Harris house, residence of the creator of Uncle Remus and Brer Rabbit. Everything about this old house was oversized. The charming ceilings were as high as in Papa's house in New Orleans, but I didn't have Amélia's sixteen-foot broom to sweep cobwebs from the high corners. In the dining room, six-foot tall windows flanked a massive fireplace, and in the spring and summer those windows were opened for ventilation.

Others had also claimed the house. Pigeons dashed themselves against the glass daily. Rather than have them kill themselves, I opened the windows each morning to watch as eight or nine of them flew into the house, roosting on the broad, high stone mantle, far above me. They bothered nothing, cooed a bit and left their calling cards beyond my reach. Each evening they flew out again, as though on signal, and we promptly closed the tall windows.

Grandmother Pauline came for a visit, and each afternoon while the children napped, she shared secrets of her early life, hoping to inspire me to write the family story, warning, "But you're not to tell these things to anyone until I'm dead and buried!" I told her I would honor her wishes; the scandals were safe with me.

The children loved getting to see her and greatly enjoyed it when she hooted like an owl when she laughed. They still imitate her, to this day. One afternoon, Grandmother gave Eddie and Randy two silver dimes and sent them to the corner store for ice cream cones; including an extra dime, for tax. She was enchanted with her great-grandsons when they bought her a little package of thumb tacks with the change. She cherished that unopened package, and carried it around in her purse, telling the story to anyone who would listen.

Jim and I drove the highways exploring the vast area surrounding Atlanta and chose a tri-level house in a modern subdivision called Doraville Southeast.

Executives with Uni-Lever, the parent company in England, came through the Atlanta office and wanted to meet us. Wining and dining them provided us the opportunity to see downtown Atlanta's fine restaurants, including Underground Atlanta. We also attended parties at Jim's supervisor's home. Jim's insecurities made him a wreck on these occasions and he became overwrought over the smallest things.

Jim admonished, "Now listen, Suga, I don't like what happened with the visiting New York manager."

"Nothing happened." I replied.

"Didn't I hear you correct him about gumbo?" he asked.

"Yes, he tried to tell me that 'filè gumbo' and 'gumbo filè' are the same thing. I cleared that up and he was delighted to learn the proper terms." I explained.

"Next time some big-wig makes a mistake, you keep your mouth shut." He demanded.

"Are you kidding? He didn't seem to mind. He even asked me to dance." I couldn't believe I was defending myself.

"Suga, your job is to sit and look pretty, nothing else. You're a corporate wife now, learn your place." He asserted.

I rejected such foolishness and spoke to whomever, about whatever I chose, and they accepted me very well.

Jim was not happy and felt stymied in an office job on Peachtree Street, instead of on the road. Atlanta was a proving ground for an even bigger promotion, and fortunately, they took three years to decide to move us again. I was relieved to have been in one place for so long. We had moved twelve times in the first ten years we were married

Moutons with Sean
Easter 1964, Atlanta

Chapter 12

All good things do come to an end, and as Jim rose in the company, he was offered a transfer to Jacksonville, Florida as a district manager. I was eager to move to the climate I knew, and a chance for the children to enjoy the beach.

It was standard procedure for the wife to be interviewed and given lots of perks to help with the relocation. Lever provided not only movers, but a preliminary trip for me, as well, to look over the area and hunt for a house. We were given a nice bonus to hire a sitter, so we went without the children. We were put up in a five-star motel where I was to spend my 30th birthday on this house-shopping trip.

Jim planned a celebration and told me he would pick me up promptly at seven o'clock after an office conference. I had my figure back and had made myself a lovely beige silk suit, had a manicure, my hair done, and waited. The phone disturbed my reverie. Jim must have been delayed. It was the front desk calling to say Mr. Mouton had a telegram. The clerk apologized, because it had come in earlier and no one had notified us. I asked if she would read it to me and I would pick it up whenever I came through the lobby. I am always afraid telegrams announce terrible news like someone's death, but I was the one who wanted to die when she read it.

"Congratulations! So happy! See you at 6:00, Signed Barb."

"Is there a last name?" I asked.

"No ma'am, just Barb." She replied. Was Barb someone who was supposed to be at his meeting?

At 6:30, I decided to pass the time and hopefully distract myself from the telegram, by reviewing the notes I had taken about the three houses I had seen. Jim wanted me to make the decision; so far, these all met our criteria, but were out of our price range. Jim was never available, so I previewed houses with an agent and told him each night what I thought would suit us.

His manager had suggested we choose, and I quote, "a large attractive house so his salesmen will be impressed when they drive their families around on Sundays. Join a country club", they told him, "entertain your men and their families."

I sat posing in the chair he would see first thing when he walked in the door, crossed my ankles 'just so' and turned on the TV. Jim had still not arrived by 8:30. I was getting hungry, so I ate a piece of cheese and fixed myself a martini.

At 9:30 I took a tranquilizer, ate crackers and another piece of cheese, fixed my lipstick, checked my hair and talked to myself in the mirror. "I'll be sweet as pie. No questions, no complaints."

I canceled our reservation at 10:30, and then at 11p.m. I took two Valiums, removed my suit, and went to bed. About daylight I heard him come in and puke in the bathroom. At breakfast, he was bleary eyed and contrite, asking to reschedule my birthday dinner. I declined and innocently asked, "Did Barb get to your meeting on time?"

He stopped eating and dropped his fork. "Barb?"

"Yes. She sent a telegram saying, 'Congratulations' and she'd see you at six, I assumed she was expected at the meeting."

"Must be some mistake. I don't know anyone named Barb. There were only men present last night. They wanted to go out for drinks and the time just got away from us." He offered.

"Right." I said.

"Don't you believe me?" he was becoming defensive.

"Jim, I'm being picked up any minute by a Century 21 agent. I have to get ready. You can pick up your telegram at the front desk." I responded, nonchalantly.

When I returned, I stopped at the desk to see if Jim had picked up the telegram. The clerk said, "Yes, Mr. Mouton came for the wire from his sister."

Jim didn't have a sister, but it was none of her business. I even kept Jim's indiscretions from the children and our friends.

The house I chose was very large. It was new, very upscale, in the developing subdivision of College Park. In the subsequent weeks, I watched as fancy furniture, more lavish than ours, came off moving vans for most of the neighbors, who were young executives with families consisting of one or two children, or none at all.

Since Jim didn't want me to take in sewing in this neighborhood, I concentrated on our children, their self-esteem, love for each other and kindness to others. I helped them write letters and taught them to share a report on the books they read. I had time to make pretty little dresses for the girls and special things for the boys. We played games together and never missed mass on Sunday.

Six months after moving to Jacksonville, Jim arrived home from a meeting, looking very sheepish. "Suga, I have bad news." Oh my God! He got somebody else pregnant? Barb?

"What kind of news?" I struggled to ask.

"I've been transferred again," he replied.

"Oh, thank God! We never could afford this showplace. You don't know how hard it's been for me to pay the bills. Six months are enough! Where are we going?" I had to ask.

"The guy in Brandon is jumping ship, going to Proctor and Gamble." He replied.

"And Brandon is where?" I asked.

"Still in Florida, a little east of Tampa." He was obviously relieved.

Eddie and Peter took moving in stride. We were all ready to go in a week. I didn't care where we lived. My children were my life and they went where Jim and I went and never complained. They learned to pack their own toys, the boys could use a magic marker to label boxes and I became a wizard at organizing a move. Help needed again, Blessed Mother! Are you still listening?

The Holiday Inn in Tampa had a dog run and allowed us to keep Sean, our gate-opening Great Dane, in our suite of rooms. This provided me great comfort, because Jim was exploring another new territory. The kids spent each day in the pool and, once again, my allowance for a sitter set me free to make the rounds with real estate agents.

I settled on a four-bedroom ranch house in Brandon near the Catholic school. Before moving, I let the kids have one last afternoon in the motel pool, and this time I went in with them. When Sean saw his mistress jump in the water, he promptly jumped in to rescue me. Good dog, but how was I supposed to get him out of the pool? There were no steps, just a ladder at each end. Dogs don't climb ladders!

I held him up, calmed him down, and convinced him I was okay. I called to several young men sunning themselves, who immediately jumped in and lifted Sean out. They introduced themselves as Brian, Carl, Dennis, Jim, and Al, from California. I thanked them, dried the children, Sean shook himself dry, and we went into our suite.

At four that afternoon, I noticed limos, full of teenage girls, deposit their riders by the side door of the motel. When the door opened they started yelling and squealing on cue. Out walked Sean's rescuers who got into another limo. The girls got back in their cars and followed. Then I recalled where I had heard those names; they were the Beach Boys, just beginning their careers in 1960.

This new house I chose had all the space we needed plus a fenced yard, a nice little one story, four-bedroom ranch type, and was only $21,000. The kids went right to school the day it opened. Missy and Suzi were still home to help unpack boxes, and I was ready to start sewing again.

The Welcome Wagon lady, introducing herself as Katie. She came with her basket of goodies and an application for the Brandon Swim and Tennis Club. There were no chairs cleared for her to sit on, so she and I sat on boxes. Before concluding her visit, the doorbell rang. I opened it to find a young woman about my age with a raw scar around her neck, looking like someone had tried to cut off her head. She had a baby boy on one hip and a plate full of frozen brownies in her hand.

"I'm Betsye" she announced, "I live across the street, down the block. I came to find out all about you."

Betsye and Katie knew each other, and we spent a good while talking.

Betsye's scar, she explained, was from recent thyroid surgery. She had seen my girls and was excited to have playmates for her 5-year old daughter, Michelle. The neighborhood children," she informed me. "had been exclusively boys, until we had arrived."

Together they briefed me on Brandon. Katie offered that it was a very small town, about 15,000 people. They said it had one stoplight, one bar, two churches, a five and dime, a dance school for the girls, and a grocery store. It also had a little clothing store which was opening a fabric store in the back.

Betsye asked, "Do you play bridge?"

"I do." I replied.

"Then you'll like the Newcomers' Club, and you'll want membership in the swim and tennis club. They're planning a golf course, too." Katie said.

The baby boy on Betsye's hip, John, was Suzi's age; they loved each other on sight, and learned to suck opposite thumbs so they could hold hands. Leslie was in Michelle's class at Nativity School.

The swim and tennis club claimed one weekend a month for big poolside theme parties. Everyone seemed to know everyone else, and Betsye's husband became our dentist. The clothing store hired me to do alterations, and I started sewing almost immediately. More importantly, we could afford to live there.

"We're going to give a black-tie party on New Year's Eve." I said to my new friends, poolside one afternoon on a balmy day in September. Suzi and John were in the wading pool.

Betsye shook her head, "I doubt you'll get anyone here to wear formal clothes especially if they have to rent a tux."

"Really? I'll make a bet with you. When word gets out, people will be begging to be invited. Trust me, it's happened before. We began doing this in New Orleans, then all the way to Atlanta; wherever we were."

Shirley, our doctor's wife said, "Bob won't wear a tux. He went to the governor's ball in a seersucker suit."

"I'll send out the invites to forty couples; those who know how to dress will come," I whispered to Betsye behind my hand.

Shirley was wrong, the doctor didn't rent a tuxedo, he bought one. Not only did we have eighty guests in our house, but for the rest of the year Jim and I were wined and dined by everyone who wanted to get on our next invitation list.

Jim was an excellent host, exuding charm and looking like a millionaire in his second tux, having worn out the first one before he finished college. He could charm the shoes off a horse.

That first winter in Brandon, Jim and I joined friends to see "Our Town" at the Tampa Community Theater. Afterwards, we met the director backstage, Sir Francis Goode, an Englishman whom we recognized from Schwepps commercials. I questioned him about starting a theater group in Brandon, which he supported wholeheartedly.

Within the week, I put a little blurb in The Brandon News and had a good crowd for Sir Francis when he came out to lecture. In no time, we assembled a board of governors and had a play in rehearsal in the high school auditorium. Unfortunately, the first performance was a failure. There were more people on the stage than in the audience. I went back to talk with Goode.

"Don't give up, it's a worthwhile cause for that charming little village you live in. Keep on trying, maybe you'll find a play people want to see."

Another ad was placed in the News for a director, and one came to the next meeting. James Roberts had only directed in college, but he wanted to branch out. Agreeing to work for nothing for a year, he directed our first financial success, "Tunnel of Love."

One of the members found us an abandoned auditorium in nearby Valrico, which could be used in exchange for a little cosmetic work. The building unused at that time so the men built sets in the daytime, we could rehearse in the evenings, and it was a success waiting to happen.

The Brandon Little Theater was born, with thirty members, support from the community, the newspaper, and an appreciative audience. We joined the Florida Theatre Conference and eventually, we had a charter. When funds allowed, we hired professionals willing to work with amateurs.

While Jim was supportive of our efforts, nobody ever expected to see him on stage. He surprised me when he landed the male lead in "Mary, Mary" a year later. The second female lead fell ill after two readings, and Cindy Butcher from Tampa was recruited to replace her. She had experience, looked right for the role as a femme fatale, and was willing to jump in.

One night during rehearsals, I was finishing up filling a cooler in the lobby when Cindy came in for the first time. The scene on stage featuring the male lead, mesmerized her and she tiptoed over to me.

"Who is that?" she whispered hungrily. "Do you know him?"

"Yes, that's Jim Mouton." I answered.

"What does he do when he's not in a play?" she inquired.

"He's a sales manager." Before I could tell her Jim was my husband, Cindy asked, "Do you know how much money he makes?"

"Come with me, Cindy." I said, "I'll introduce you to the director," ignoring her question, I then shuffled her through the dark auditorium.

Cindy started bringing her 5-year old twins, expecting them to sit in the cold, dark rehearsal hall until very late. Their daycare provider had them in their pajamas when Cindy had picked them up after work. Who knows what they ate? They were Suzi's age, so I offered to let Cindy drop them at our house on her way to rehearsals. I fed them with my kids and put them to bed. Most often it was after midnight when she picked them up. Why are they rehearsing so late, I wondered?

I soon caught on to Cindy and Jim's game. Rehearsals actually ended about 9:30; something else was taking up two and a half hours of their time. When my suspicions wouldn't rest, I engaged a sitter and followed them straight to the trailer Jim had rented, supposedly to conduct interviews. She then would pick up her twins, alone. Much as I hated to put these innocent babies out, I told Cindy after a week, to make other arrangements. They were literally using me to enable their affair and I refused to cooperate.

At the age of 32, after six pregnancies, my body was spent. My teeth were drained of calcium, my hair was thinning, and I was exhausted and in constant pain. Betsye introduced me to Dr. Dave, her OB/GYN, who determined a hysterectomy was necessary. I would be incapacitated for a month, I was told.

Jim arranged for the two boys to stay with his parents; my brother, Jerry, and his wife, Sunny, took the two big girls, and the two little ones went to Auntie Rosie. The trick was to get them all from Florida to Louisiana while school was out.

Betsye offered to share the driving and provide moral support on the trip. The plan was to drive all night, now with my six children plus her three. Our guardian angels worked overtime during that Sunday escapade from Brandon to New Orleans; six hundred and fifty miles in twelve hours. After they were fed, the kids were bedded down on quilts in the back of my station wagon and slept straight through without a problem.

Shortly after daylight, we pulled into Rosie's driveway and Suzi was the last to tumble out, landing face down on the concrete. Her two upper front teeth were knocked loose. I was quick to get on the phone. Using Jim's fraternity roster, I found Greg Kyle, DDS, who saw Suzi immediately. He reassured me that these were baby teeth and, hopefully, permanent teeth would grow in when expected.

Betsye and I had an uneventful return trip home on Wednesday, in daylight, with just her three children. I felt lost without my brood, knowing it would be a month before I saw them again.

My hysterectomy was scheduled for Thursday. Betsye was more than a friend, she was an RN, and stayed overnight with me for the first two days. All seemed to be going well. By Sunday, I was feeling fine, and Jim was in town, due to visit me. He came up to my room at 12:45 p.m., only to tell me that Cindy had invited him over for lunch at one o'clock.

"Jim," I cried," I can't believe you won't spend even a little time with me."

"Suga, be reasonable. I rented you a TV and you have a lovely view. What more can I do for you? And before you answer, I'm going anyway." He justified his actions by saying, "I could have just told you on the phone, but I came all the way up to the hospital. Get hold of yourself and dig into your lunch tray here."

"No! I've been alone, just waiting for you." I cried.

"I'm sorry, Suga, I'm leaving now." He turned on his heels and left.

I was aghast. I grabbed a metal salad bowl off my tray and threw it at the door, making a mess and a racket. I pulled out my IV, got out of bed, got into my dress and woozily headed to the elevators. When I got out in the lobby, I was crying, and the guard at the door asked, "Ma'am, are you all right?"

"Please call me a taxi." I sniffed.

I didn't have a cent. When the cab pulled up I got in, giving the driver my address. The house was empty and unlocked, so the driver waited while I went in and found money to pay him. I then staggered down the hall and crawled into the bottom bunk in the boys' room and fell asleep, still heavily drugged.

The hospital had notified Dr. Dave when they discovered my absence; he called Betsye and asked her to check my house. I woke up to her kneeling beside the bed shouting at me. "Lynne! Wake up. Are you crazy? How could you do this to me? You can bleed to death, you idiot! I tried so hard to help and this is how you repay me? You're going back to the hospital, right now. I already called for an ambulance."

I was kept an extra week in a room on the 4th floor where I was locked in. I didn't see Jim until I was discharged.

Three weeks later, Jerry and Sunny returned Jane and Leslie to us, but the boys were still with Jim's parents, and Missy and Suzi stayed at Auntie Rosie's.

Jim drove me and the two big girls to a beach house where I could recuperate. The house belonged to one of his salesmen and was rarely used. We drove through Ft. Myers, over a causeway to Sanibel's sixteen winding miles of sea grape and waving palms. I could smell the briny scent of the water but didn't see the Gulf until we crossed over to Captiva Island. He settled us in the small white clapboard house, said goodbye to the kids but not a word to me.

We had packed lots of food, bathing suits and towels, and I spent a delightful month sitting at the water's edge reading a book behind the house. I sat on the beach for hours as the gulf spit curly waves around my feet and the girls picked up pretty shells. Next door, the McCauls offered the girls expert advice identifying their treasures from the sea.

We spent lazy afternoons taking long walks, listening to the song of the surf and imagining what it was telling us. Some days they wore themselves out in the water. As we turned pink, then tan, we dug around looking for the treasure that was rumored to be buried there; we also read that the pirate, Gaspirilla, kept his captive women on this island I made colorful miniature sarongs for them and we pretended to be those beautiful captives. Encouraging play-acting kept the children uninhibited.

It all ended too soon. On the last day, I stood on the warm beach at daylight watching the calm surf wash over the flat sand, eager to see Jim, whom I still loved despite his disloyalty. In no uncertain terms, I couldn't spend another day without my two boys and two baby girls.

It was time to start breakfast before Jane and Leslie's pretty, sleepy little faces wandered into the kitchen. While I did that, I ticked off in my mind the things the girls brought that we'd have to gather before we were picked up. When Jim arrived, he loaded up the car, and as soon as the girls nodded off, he told me his news.

"Now, Suga, don't expect our lives to be the same. I won't be having sex with you again. You're not a whole woman anymore." I was astounded. This sounds like something his frigid mother had put in his head. How serious could he be?

"Do I have anything to say about that?" I asked.

"Not after the way you behaved in the hospital. You killed anything I ever felt for you." Jim replied righteously.

I took all this in. Lever Brothers focus was on families, and they frowned at divorces. He still needed a presentable wife, so he wasn't going to leave me. We still had a social calendar filled with business functions, and I was well regarded by his management team. Jane would turn 7-years old, enter the first grade and make her first communion. He was a prominent member of our parish and would certainly be involved. We had already discussed celebrating her big occasion by taking the children out for lunch at The Columbia Restaurant in Ybor City, where he could show off his family with pride. Plus, he was a scout master and president of the PTA.

I relaxed, closed my eyes as the highway led us home, and began designing in my head, starting with new matching outfits for the kids. His declaration was ho-hum to me, I would just bide my time.

At the swim club functions, Jim was always "on" like a politician. He danced with all the ladies, seldom with me, even though I had made an excellent dancer of him. Everybody loved 'Mr. Congeniality' He drank a lot, but so did everyone else, and Jim was always the last one to leave.

Having seen enough during one of these functions, I said goodnight and simply walked the few blocks home. Hours later Jim showed up without a key and I met him at the door. He reeked of booze.

"Why'd you leave?" he asked.

"Was I supposed to enjoy watching you dancing with Jackie and slobbering all over her?" I replied angrily.

"You're jealous." He swayed and belched.

"She's way out of your league, Jim." I retorted.

He charged at me with a closed fist shouting, "I'll knock your head off before I let you tell me what to do!" He punched me in the sternum and I fell over a rattan chair in the living room. While I was on the floor he kept pounding me with both fists, so I put my arms up to take the blows. When he paused, I struggled to my feet; we paced all over the room, like a pair of wrestlers. Suddenly, he stopped and pulled off his shirt and pants, throwing them aside. I grabbed the belt out of his slacks, and doubling it, swung it at him, getting in one good blow to his shoulder.

Jim then turned away and dashed through the patio slider leading out to the back porch. I quickly locked it and ran through the dining room to the other glass doors, locking them also. He was stuck out on the porch, in his underwear.

I took my time, checking on the children to make sure they were still sleeping, then I opened the window over the sink to see where he was. He had passed out on the daybed directly below the kitchen window and was snoring. I filled my largest pot with cold water, and with a super-human effort, raised it over the windowsill, and poured it on him. He was so far gone it didn't wake him. I laughed and went to bed.

The next morning, he stood outside the glass door shouting at me to let him in. If I didn't let him in the back, he would have to go out through the yard around to the front door where the neighbors would see him. I poked my head out the window over the sink.

"What's the matter, Jim?" I asked innocently.

"Let me in, Suga, I think I wet the bed." He replied morosely.

The kids woke up; Eddie came out of his room and seeing his father, unlocked the sliding door. Jim stormed in and took a long time in the shower. When he came into the kitchen he saw the bruises on my face and arms, and asked, "What the hell happened to you? I didn't do that to you, I would remember if I hurt you. I don't even remember coming home. Man, have I got a hangover!"

"I hit you, too, Jim, and I'm sorry. Maybe we should discuss this some other time." The children were listening, and I wasn't going to upset them. I wore long sleeves for a month, and life went on as usual.

Jim seemed to be pleased with life in Brandon until the third year. I noticed that on Sundays he didn't receive communion, nor did he go to confession with the children and me on Saturdays but kept up his image by going to mass.

"Is there something you want to tell me, Jim?" I asked carefully.

"No Suga, I'd have a hard time talking about it. I can't face you anymore." He said miserably.

"What did I do?" I asked.

"Nothing, I just, I ...you know... you've known all along what a louse I've been. I've confessed my affairs and you forgave me, you never bring them up." He said.

I remembered the priest in Houston and his words flashed through my brain, "**Never, ever bring it up**."

"What good would it have done?" I asked.

"It's just that I know what you're thinking, and I can't face you anymore. I'm moving out. I'm sorry, I'm done." He stated with finality.

"No! What about our family?" Desperately searching for a solution, I racked my brain.

Counseling? We have such a beautiful family, what can we do? I needed to allay his guilt somehow.

"Listen Jim," I said, "if it's guilt that's killing you, would you feel better if I told you I've been cheating, too? Sleeping around, I mean." His face turned red and he went into a rage.

"Who? Who did you sleep with? Where?" he demanded.

"Oh, I don't know, just guys, anybody who wanted me, everywhere we've lived."

Jim made a fist. “You’re lying. You’re making this up.”

“Don’t hit me.” I ducked away as he punched the wall behind me. “Yes! I made it up trying to make you feel better! I don’t want you to leave! Let’s try to work it out.”

“Goddammit, Suga, Now I’ll never know what to believe. I’ll never be able to trust you again!” he shouted. His fist was obviously hurt, the knuckles bleeding all over. He had never been able to find a stud when he wanted to hang a picture. That night he punched one. Jim left, furiously slamming the door. As the X-ray revealed, all his knuckles were broken on his right hand.

I wanted to hold on to the vows we had made, the love we once had. I was determined to keep my family intact. Jim only came over on Saturdays to bring the children their allowances. No one on the street realized he wasn’t living at home because his car had so seldom been there anyway. He did agree to see a marriage counselor. Dashing in one day just in time to pick me up for an appointment, he asked if I would drive. We had little to say to each other on the way downtown until Jim asked, “How much longer are we going to do this?”

“I guess until we can resolve our issues,” I replied.

“Suga, there is no resolution. I just go each week and say what he wants to hear.” He admitted.

“You have to be kidding.” I said, approaching a major intersection where I cruised to a stop. “You’re telling me you’re just playing along?”

He nodded.

“Get out!” I demanded.

Horns were blaring, the light changed, but I refused to move.

He was incredulous, shouting, “I can’t get out here!”

“I mean it. **Get out!** I’m not moving this car until you do.” I shouted back.

He gave me a look sharper than a guillotine blade and got out. Rush hour commuters were honking and yelling. He shouted over the din, “You’ll hear from my lawyer.” He slammed the door, and I drove on, leaving him standing on the median with cars whizzing by.

I knew the children needed to see Jim, so I arranged to visit Betsye's new house on Sunday afternoons, giving him use of the house to spend time with them. I told seven-year-old Jane where I was going and gave her Betsye's number in case she needed me. Sooner than expected Jane called. "Mom, that lady's here."

"What lady?" I asked.

"The one who was in the play with Dad. He locked us in the back of the house. She took off her panty hose and threw them on the floor! Mom, I don't think that's right. Leslie and Missy are crying and Suzi's about to start."

"I'll be right there." I assured her.

I grabbed my keys and drove home at breakneck speed. Both Jim and Cindy's cars were in the driveway. Using my key, I opened the door, catching Jim and Cindy in a clinch. Of course, they were shocked to see me when I burst in on them.

"Suga!" Jim said hoarsely, "we're rehearsing! What are you doing back here?"

"Don't be ridiculous, I know you're not in another play. You, Cindy, get out of my house and take him with you!"

She only looked at him, saying not a word. He handed Cindy her jacket and she headed quickly for the door. I pointed to him. "You go, too! Get out of here with your tramp!" Jim sheepishly followed Cindy out.

I picked up the panty hose and threw them out the door. "And take your dirty underwear!" Shaking all over, I then turned, rushing to unlock the children confined in the back room.

He's gone, I thought, really gone. Gone for good. How much of this is my fault? I went into the bedroom and grabbed up his Loyola graduation picture, throwing it with all my strength through the open closet door where his suits once hung. It smashed against the back wall.

The children were in bed when he came in January for his suitcases and his last two garment bags. All the details of his move were settled, and he had filed for divorce. When he told me what his grounds were, I laughed.

His plan was to tell the magistrate that I had served him red beans and rice once a week for thirteen years, and that he didn't like red beans and rice. I begged him not to make a fool of himself saying something so absurd. In Louisiana, everyone grows up eating this traditional dish, beans and rice made with ham hocks! But this was all he could come up with. He didn't even need that. Florida is a no-fault state; one needs only to say that the parties are no longer compatible.

Jim and I agreed to remain on good terms for the children. He asked to spend one last night in the house, since it was so late. For the last time, we went to bed together. During the night, I felt his hands moving over my body and I didn't resist. Within a few minutes he had satisfied himself and I realized he was asleep, snoring. Nothing had changed since our honeymoon.

I got up at 6 a.m., made coffee, and got the boys and the two big girls off to school after their breakfast. They walked the few short blocks carrying lunch boxes and school bags, Jane holding Leslie's hand, as usual.

I heard the shower go off in our bathroom. A few minutes later Jim came out of the bedroom, shaved and dressed. He walked through the den to the breakfast bar, got his coffee and without looking at me, he said, "About last night." he sipped his coffee. He was so close I could smell his Old Spice.

"Yes?" I shrugged.

"It didn't mean anything." He said.

"Oh. Does this mean you want your fraternity pin back?" I asked sarcastically.

"Nobody likes a smart ass, Suga." He picked up his briefcase, heading abruptly for the door.

Missy came dashing out of her bedroom, trying to reach him. She was too little and too late. As the door slammed in her face she turned to me, big tears welling up in her eyes.

"Daddy??"

Both Jim and I had, for three years, encouraged the boys when they joined the corps of altar boys. We were truly proud when they finally earned their way onto the altar, serving mass. When Peter came home alone one Saturday following altar boy practice, I was afraid Eddie has gotten into some trouble. Almost a half hour later I heard his bike roll in to the drive and drop onto the concrete. He came through the garage, into the house, passing me in the kitchen without a word. I could see he had been crying. He headed for his room and wouldn't look at me.

"Hi, darlin', did you have a good practice?" I asked. He looked away. "Come here, son, Mom is speaking to you. What's wrong?"

"Father Sweeny said I can't tell you," he replied stubbornly.

My heart felt like a stone tossed down a well. "You can tell me anything. Did Father do something to you?"

I could see he was conflicted, wanting to tell me, but obviously had been given firm warning not to.

"I'm going to ask you to break whatever promise you made to Father Sweeny and let me help you." I held out my arms and my devastated ten-year old came right into my embrace. He had trouble talking with the strangle of tears he was fighting. I grew more frightened and cold.

The others were outside in the back yard setting up for a picnic and dusting off the wooden table and the Big Apple grill. I sat down at the kitchen table and urged Eddie to sit with me. I held his two hands. He was still avoiding my eyes, embarrassed and sobbing.

"Did Father Sweeny touch you, Eddie?" I asked gently.

"No, Mom." He was struggling with composure. "He told me that you and Dad are going to hell and it's my fault."

"What!? We're not going to hell!" I was stunned.

"He says you're both going to get married again eventually, and you'll end in hell. He says it's my job to stop you and if I don't, I'll go to hell, too!" A new rush of tears. He was devastated. I simply hugged him.

"We'll see about this." I tried to comfort him.

Jim's car was pulling into the driveway for his ritual Saturday visit. I sent Eddie out into the yard with the others and told Jim what he had said. Without a word, Jim got back in his car and headed down the street toward the rectory. I brought out buns and a tray of hot dogs and hamburgers and tried to act as though nothing had happened.

"Look lively, kids," I said, Dad's coming with your allowances, and maybe he'll sit down and have a bite with us." I let the boys use the tongs on the meats; Leslie and Jane put mustard and mayonnaise on the table, and Suzi and Missy laid out pickles and chips on the paper plates.

Before long Jim returned, greeted his enthusiastic family, giving the kids quarters, nickels and dimes for their weekly allowance. After we ate, I moved closer to Jim while he tossed the ball back and forth to Peter.

"Did you see him?" I asked.

To which Jim replied, "Oh, yeah." He threw the ball.

"And?" I was anxious.

"I just told Sweeny that if he ever so much as spoke to any Mouton child again, we would be putting flowers on his grave and sending a sympathy card to his mother in Ireland."

Life goes on. What does the future hold?

After thirteen years of building my life around suiting my husband's needs, I found myself supremely independent. I was single but not alone. I had my six beautiful, creative and resilient children.

"Lynne has the talent to bring the reader into her story and long for more."

Mary Ann Revell, Educator

"Refined Suga spans a lifetime of inspiration and generosity. It is truly a magical journey of unconditional love."

Jane Kreisman Soslow, Owner of Gramps Books
Author, Editor, Educator

DON'T MISS THE NEXT TWO INSTALLMENTS IN THE SERIES!

Hey, Lady!

Book two brings more children for Lynne to raise, relocation to Sanibel and Captiva Islands, a devastating fire, stage and film credits for herself and the children, and the tragic loss of a husband.

The French Resolution

Lynne's third book tells of grief over the loss of a child and provides an end to her struggle to resolve the identity of her parents. Readers are provided a look into her reign as Queen of Mardi Gras and a surprise visitor reveals how the kids managed to melt her license plate in her garage without damaging the car!

There is talk of a fourth book!

97152625R00089

Made in the USA
Columbia, SC
13 June 2018